PRAISE FOR
The BE BRAVE ACTIVITY BOOK

"This book is a great book for kids, parents, and psychologists. Dr. Kathryn knows how to make being brave and working hard fun! If you follow this book, you are going to be a really brave kid."

—**Henry Biebl**, fourth grader and book lover

"As a child psychologist, I'm always on the lookout for resources that can help families. I love how this workbook explains exposure therapy using kid-friendly language and relatable examples. The interactive exercises make tackling anxiety feel less scary and more like a fun game. This is a fantastic tool for parents, therapists, and kids battling anxiety."

—**Rebecca Schneider, PhD**, assistant professor and director of the Child OCD Program at Emory University School of Medicine

"Dr. Hecht has filled a significant void in the field by writing a book tailored for families of children with OCD or anxiety and the therapists treating them. What is most impressive about Dr. Hecht's book is the focus—in a fun, user-friendly manner—on core, evidence-based treatment ingredients that are known to promote recovery from OCD and anxiety. The text is comprehensive and applicable for children with a range of anxiety and OCD concerns, and it is sure to help readers of all types (kids, their loved ones, and therapists) to translate key therapeutic concepts into real-life improved outcomes."

—**Eric A. Storch, PhD**, McIngvale Presidential Endowed Chair and professor, Department of Psychiatry and Behavioral Sciences at Baylor College of Medicine

"This book has the holy grail ability to hold both the #1 spot on my recommended reading list for parents of anxious children *and* my 'Clinicians Must Use' list. Each artistic page guides kids through the most effective model of anxiety treatment with all the steps spelled out. Most books on anxiety are overly reliant on 'coping strategies' rather than on the active ingredient of pediatric anxiety—behavioral exposures. Dr. Hecht's expertise guides readers through *real* exposure therapy and demystifies the art of approaching fears to dissolve anxiety once and for all."

—**Jessica Bodie, PhD**, director of child services at the Center for the Treatment and Study of Anxiety at the University of Pennsylvania

"This book is brilliant. I recommend it for both parents supporting children in overcoming their fears and therapists looking for novel exposure ideas. This book is the perfect blend of fun with evidence-based knowledge."

—**Maria Fraire, PhD**, program director of the OCD Institute for Children & Adolescents, McLean Hospital/Harvard Medical School

"This is a practical workbook that helps children and families understand and overcome fear and anxiety through a series of fun and engaging activities. It's a must-have resource for families and therapists."

—**Joseph F. McGuire, PhD,** James C. Harris professor in developmental neuropsychiatry and neurosciences research, Division of Child & Adolescent Psychiatry, Department of Psychiatry & Behavioral Sciences at Johns Hopkins University School of Medicine

"Dr. Kathryn makes exposure work *fun* with this practical toolkit—sure to empower kids struggling with anxiety and become a clinician's best friend when planning exposed-based activities! Finally, a fun tool kit to help kick-start brave work for kids struggling with anxiety!

—**Alison Newcomer PhD,** licensed clinical psychologist and pediatric anxiety specialist

THE BE BRAVE ACTIVITY BOOK
Copyright © 2025 by Kathryn F. Hecht

Published by
PESI Publishing, Inc.
3839 White Ave
Eau Claire, WI 54703

Cover and interior design by Emily Dyer
Illustrations by Kathryn F. Hecht, PhD
Editing by Jenessa Jackson, PhD

ISBN 9781683736905 (print)
ISBN 9781683736912 (ePUB)
ISBN 9781683736929 (ePDF)

All rights reserved.
Printed in the United States of America.

In every dinosaur rescued,
blanket fort conquered,
and spider king vanquished,
you show me the point
where brave meets fun.

**To Juniper and Olive,
with all my love.**

Table of Contents

A Letter to Caring Adults ix

A Letter to Kids xi

What's in This Chapter | **Fancy Name**

1. QUICK-START GUIDE 1
2. SOCIAL STUFF .... Social Anxiety 15
3. SCHOOL STUFF .... School Anxiety 30
4. DOING STUFF ALONE .... Separation Anxiety 46
5. (IM)PERFECTION AND MISTAKEZ .... Perfectionism 63
6. SPOOKY STUFF .... Phobias 84
7. GROSS STUFF .... Contamination Fears 101
8. IMAGINATION GONE WILD .... Intrusive Thoughts 120
9. FUNNY FEELINGS .... Panic 141
10. CRINGEY STUFF .... Embarrassment 164
11. NOT KNOWING STUFF .... Uncertainty 187

Conclusion 205

Appendix 209

About the Author 221

Disclaimer

There are, of course, real risks associated with the exposure-based activities in this book. Just like when you take your child swimming at a public pool, buckle them into a car for a drive, drop them off for their first sleepover, or even let go of those tiny hands so they can take their first steps alone, there are things that can go wrong. Only you know the specific circumstances of your family, your personal parental risk tolerance, and your child's current health and capabilities, so please review the activities in this book carefully. If there are challenges that you feel your child should not try for any reason, feel free to skip them or save them for some time down the road.

However, in your risk assessment, please also remember that part of developing resilience is experiencing things that go less than perfect, or even downright poor, and learning that we can handle the outcome. Muscles get stronger only when they are stretched and stressed through exercise, and bones get stronger only when they are asked to bear the weight of our bodies. Children are the same—they are "antifragile," needing challenge in order to gain confidence in their own capacity. A little struggle can go a long way toward a child knowing they can handle hard stuff and being willing to take the risks necessary to live a full, fabulous life.

A Letter to Caring Adults

If you were offered a magic wand to guarantee the course of a child's development, what would you wish for? My guess is that, like most parents, therapists, and other caring adults, you would wish for your child or client to develop into a healthy, well-adjusted, and confident individual who will eventually grow up, go off into the world, and pursue exactly what they want to do. We all wish a fabulous and rich life for our kids, one filled with magic and meaning.

Does this mean we wish for kids who never ever get anxious? Of course not! Anxiety is adaptive, helping us avoid harm and make smart choices about risk. In fact, research has taught us that anxiety can even enhance our performance if we can find the sweet spot. (Don't believe me? Google "Yerkes-Dodson curve.") However, those of us who provide treatment for anxiety know that kids who allow their Worry (yes, with a capital W) to call *all* the shots will end up in a smaller and smaller world, because Worry's go-to advice is to avoid anything where safety and comfort cannot be guaranteed. (And spoiler: When it comes to anything that hasn't happened yet, safety and comfort can *never* be guaranteed.)

Instead, we want kids to gain confidence in their competence. To learn that anxiety is both tolerable and temporary. To feel, deep in their bones, that they have the ability to handle the uncertainties and imperfections in life, and any worry that comes along with it.

How do we help kids achieve this? The same way we learn anything else: through practice doing hard or challenging things. As a child clinical psychologist who specializes in the treatment of anxiety, obsessive-compulsive disorder (OCD), and related issues, I have worked with hundreds of children and adolescents to successfully tackle their worries and fears using cognitive behavioral therapy (CBT). My aim in writing this book is to provide mental health professionals, trainees, and parents with the tools that make it easy and fun to deliver the "active ingredient" in CBT for anxiety: exposure.

When it comes to anxiety, OCD, and related issues, exposure-based CBT is the gold standard of treatment. With this approach, children learn to overcome their fears by intentionally "exposing" themselves to the thoughts and situations that provoke discomfort. Fifty years of research and numerous randomized controlled trials support exposure as the most powerful ingredient in the behavioral treatment of anxiety. Not only can exposure-based treatment actually rewire an anxious brain, but it can change key neurotransmitter levels the same way that medications do. For these reasons, exposure-based CBT is currently a first-line treatment (a.k.a. the first thing to try) for pediatric anxiety and OCD, recommended by both the American Academy of Child and Adolescent Psychiatry and the Society of Clinical Child and Adolescent Psychology.

Despite this robust evidence base, exposure remains an underutilized tool in many pediatric anxiety treatment toolboxes, and it is an often unfamiliar (and uncomfortable!) concept for parents interested in supporting their anxious child. Therapists I have trained in exposure treatment frequently struggle with how to introduce the concept of exposure to children, how to get families on board, and how to make this inherently uncomfortable process as fun as possible. It can also be a struggle to come up with exposure or "brave challenge" ideas. Even those of us specializing in anxiety treatment—myself included!—will at times get stuck trying to come up with creative, effective, and empowering exposures for a motivated child.

This book addresses these challenges by providing a curated suite of exposure ideas that focus on the most common types of pediatric anxiety, with built-in tools and tracking logs that ensure each challenge is the most effective learning opportunity it can be.

To orient your child to the concept of exposure, the first chapter provides a quick-start guide on the basics of CBT for anxiety—it's everything you need to know about how Worry works in 10 minutes or less. This chapter lays out some of the cognitive distortions, or "tricks," that Worry tends to use to get kids feeling worse than they need to. It also covers the "big secret" about anxiety—that doing what Worry says and avoiding your fears will make you feel better at first but more anxious over time, while doing the opposite and facing your fears (a.k.a. exposure!) is the path to feeling better. You'll also find instructions on how to tailor the challenges in this book for your child and how to build a "Bravery Ladder" to help them work their way up to too-tricky-for-now challenges.

The subsequent chapters each focus on a flavor of anxiety that is common over the course of childhood. In each chapter, you'll find an overview of that specific type of anxiety, some considerations to keep in mind when helping kids face that particular fear, and 10 or more unique exposure exercises you can use with kids—whether you're a clinician working with a young client on bravery-building skills or a parent looking to support their anxious child. Throughout each chapter, you'll also find "Pro Tip" sections that provide you with suggestions and tricks for how to best support your kid when they're working to face their fears.

One final note: Please remember that the goal of these challenges is not to get rid of your child's anxiety once and for all. Remember, anxiety is normal and adaptive—we expect it to show up when doing the things we care about! The goal is also not for your child to complete each activity with no distress. Rather, the goal is for your child to practice *handling* anxiety—that is, letting it show up and pass without avoiding or changing their behavior. Being able to tolerate anxiety and make it through a challenging situation—even if it doesn't go perfectly and even if it's not totally comfortable—is called *coping efficacy*, or what I call "handleability." Coping efficacy is an important predictor of symptom reduction during anxiety treatment. It seems that helping kids build up their confidence in their ability to handle it—whatever "it" may be—is key to ensuring that anxiety stops getting in the way. You want your kids to be able to make a plan and do what matters to them—Pet the dog! Ride the ride! Give the speech!—*despite* any anxiety that shows up.

So . . . that fabulous future of magic and meaning we want for our kids, that Big Brave Life? It's in reach, and exposure is our magic wand. Let's get waving.

A Letter to Kids

ALERT! This book might get you dirty. You might end up kind of cold, or a little wet. You might end up covered in paint, or up in a tree, or surrounded by kittens. This book might take you somewhere you have never been before, with people you have never met. This book might get you a little squirmy, taking you juuust outside what feels comfortable. You might not always love it.

But this book might also get you excited. Energized. Feeling *proud*. Because this book will get you BRAVE.

This book is called *The Be Brave Activity Book*. Lots of kids think that being brave means you don't get scared. But it's really the opposite—it is IMPOSSIBLE to be brave without fear.

Think about a knight going off to rescue a king from a dragon. If the knight thinks fighting the dragon will be safe, no big deal, chill, a casual Tuesday activity, would we think the knight is brave? No! We would think the knight is dumb.

But if the knight understands the risks, feels afraid, and then goes off to fight the dragon and rescue the king even though that knight is not sure how it will go . . . that's being brave.

Brave is feeling nervous about something, not knowing for sure how it will go, and then doing it anyway.

Brave is not comfortable. Brave is not always easy, either. **But Brave is worth it, because Brave means that even if that old trickster Worry shows up, you still get to do what matters to you, since you *know* you can handle whatever life throws at you.**

So . . . are you ready to have a few adventures, step outside your comfort zone, and become that superhero known as a Braver Kid? Let's go! Lots of high fives ahead, I just know it.

Happy bravery building,

—DR. KATHRYN

CHAPTER 1
Quick-Start Guide

Welcome, friend! I'm so glad you are here. Impressed, too. Because if you are here, that means that you are one of those clever kids who is so tuned in to how you are feeling that you have noticed anxiety lurking around. If you are reading this, I bet you have also noticed how annoying anxiety can be. If Worry drives you crazy sometimes, I have good news: This workbook will help.

I'm Dr. Kathryn, a psychologist and kid anxiety specialist, and I'm here to be your guide in tackling anxiety. Before we start with all that though, let me be clear: **Anxiety. Is. NORMAL.** Every person on planet Earth worries sometimes . . . or, let's be honest, a lot of the time! But anxiety can also stop you from doing all kinds of things you might want to do, from going to a birthday party to trying out for a team. It can suck the fun out of even the funnest activities, especially if a spooky thought gets a good grip on your brain at the wrong time. When anxiety starts to get in the way of Maximum Fun, it's time to do something about it.

This book is packed full of activities that will help shrink anxiety down and take scary stuff from a shriek to a shrug. However, in order to do this, you'll need to know a bit about your opponent first and then learn the three big secrets about Worry. I promise, I'll keep it short . . .

Your Opponent: Who Are You Dealing With?

First, let's take that spooky voice out of your head and get it on paper. **Those anxious thoughts are Worry talking.** That's right, Worry with a capital W. When you imagine Worry, what does it look like? Is it a monster? A fluffball? A tiny, nervous toddler?

This is how Dr. Kathryn draws her worry.

Go ahead and draw Worry here, and while you're at it, give your character a name. The name can be plain old Worry, Anxiety with a capital A, or something a little silly, like Be-Sure Bob, Exaggerating Eddie, Dr. Doom, or Sassy Sally.

Well done! Now that you know who you are dealing with, you need to know what Worry is saying. Tune in and listen to what Worry says about the people, places, or situations that you fear. What does Worry predict will happen? Is it maybe something not so good, or is it pretty uncomfortable? Does Worry say that if something goes wrong, it would be a capital-letter BIG DEAL? Maybe that you couldn't possibly handle the not-so-good thing happening?

Write Worry's predictions here:

2 • **The Be Brave Activity Book**

When Worry makes a spooky prediction like this, your brain automatically turns on your body's emergency response system (a.k.a. the sympathetic nervous system). This emergency response system is called the *fight-or-flight response* because everything that happens in your body is gearing you up to either fight something dangerous or run away.

Early warning signs: Which of these feelings do you notice first when you are anxious? Put a check mark by them below:

☆ Your breathing and heart rate get faster, allowing more oxygen to get to your muscles and letting you run faster and longer.

☆ You start to sweat, which is your body's air conditioning system. This keeps those tense muscles cool so you can fight or run for a longer time.

☆ Your muscles get tense and twitchy, giving you lightning-fast reflexes.

☆ Your body pulls the emergency brake on your digestion because turning food into fuel takes a ton of energy. When digestion stops, it can give way to tummy troubles or butterflies in your stomach, but it frees up a lot of energy for your running and fighting muscles.

The fight-or-flight response is great if there's real danger in front of you. It basically turns you into a superhero warrior, ready to take on a snarling tiger or boss-level bad guy!

However, sometimes, this alarm system gets activated when there's no danger. When the fight-or-flight response kicks in because you're worrying about something that might (or might not) happen, you get False Alarm Feelings. Everything feels exactly the same as if you were facing that tiger . . . but there's no real danger right now.

If you notice that your alarm system is turning on and there's no tiger in front of you, it's a clue to tune into what Worry is saying, because here's the first big secret about Worry . . .

SECRET #1: WORRY IS A TRICKSTER

Even though it seems like Worry is just trying to be helpful and keep you safe, it usually ends up tricking kids into feeling worse than they need to. Why? Because Worry is constantly telling fibs. There are many types of Worry fibs, and I could fill up a whole book telling you all of Worry's tricks, but since this is a quick-start guide, let's focus on the BIG THREE.

If you took the most common Worry tricks and made a Worry's Greatest Hits album, the songs that would top the charts are:

 THE VERY UNLIKELY BAD NEWS BLUES: Worry says that something terrible is going to happen, even though that thing is very, very unlikely, or even impossible.

This is called CATASTROPHIZING.

fancy name: MAGNIFICATION

#2 THE OH-NO MAGNIFYING GLASS: Worry makes something not so good seem way worse than it actually is.

Also called INCAPABILITY.

 THE CAN'T-HANDLE KID: Worry says that you can't handle a situation that you actually *can* handle just fine.

Look back at the Worry thoughts you wrote down or created on page 2. Do you see any of these tricks at play? Go ahead and make a note if you do. And a little tip: Sometimes Worry will use more than one trick in the same thought! If you are having trouble figuring out Worry's tricks on your own, feel free to snag a grown-up as a teammate on this one.

That dog will DEFINITELY bite you!

Hmm... Puddles has never done that before... ever. Seems like The Very Unlikely Bad News Blues trick.

4 • The Be Brave Activity Book

Oh, and let me guess: Worry is also telling you that, in order to prevent that bad thing from happening, you have to AVOID that thing, because that's the only way to be SURE you will be safe.

What are some of the things Worry tells you to avoid doing? Check the boxes below:

- ☐ Don't talk to that person you don't know.
- ☐ Don't ask that new friend to play.
- ☐ Don't tell a joke in a group.
- ☐ Don't go to school.
- ☐ Don't ask a question in class.
- ☐ Don't give a presentation.
- ☐ Don't do anything where you might be judged.
- ☐ Don't go high up.
- ☐ Don't pet that dog.
- ☐ Don't do anything where you might get hurt.
- ☐ Don't let your family do anything where THEY might get hurt.
- ☐ Don't stay home alone.
- ☐ Don't go to bed alone.
- ☐ Don't let your parents go away from you.
- ☐ Don't go in the basement.
- ☐ Don't go out in the dark.
- ☐ Don't make any mistakes.
- ☐ Don't try something you could fail at.
- ☐ Don't try new foods you might not like.
- ☐ Don't play a game where you might get too cold, hot, dizzy, or sweaty.
- ☐ Don't touch that gross thing.
- ☐ Don't be around anything that might gross you out.
- ☐ Don't do anything that might make you sick or throw up.
- ☐ Don't ride that roller coaster.
- ☐ Don't do anything weird or silly in front of others.
- ☐ Don't dance in front of others.
- ☐ Don't sing in front of others.
- ☐ Don't let yourself think that scary thought.
- ☐ Don't go to sleep in case you have a bad dream.
- ☐ Don't leave it to chance—ask a parent to be sure.
- ☐ Other: _____

Check out that list—did you notice that every single one of the things that Worry is telling you to do is a command? Do this! Don't do that! Do what I say, or else!

This brings us to the second big secret . . .

My my! Worry is DEMANDING.

 # WORRY IS BOSSY

Worry desperately wants you to do exactly as it says, every single time, no exceptions, and it will try very hard to boss you around all day long. And, just like when you let a bully boss you around, each time you follow Worry's commands, you give it a bit more power over you. Worry might leave you alone *for now* after you do what it says, but eventually, it will be back for more . . . and it will usually start to ask for even more too.

Let's say that Worry tells you that dogs aren't safe ("Don't pet that dog!"). After a while, it won't be enough to just avoid the big, grumpy dog that lives down the block. Soon, Worry will tell you that to *really* be safe, you have to avoid every big dog . . . then also those medium-sized dogs . . . and eventually, any dog at all.

Doing what Worry says might feel good in the short term, because when you avoid something that feels scary, the scary feelings go away. You get instant relief! At least for a while . . . but over time, when you do what Worry says, it only makes the Worry grow bigger and bigger—and before you know it, that trickster will become bigger and louder and bossier than ever.

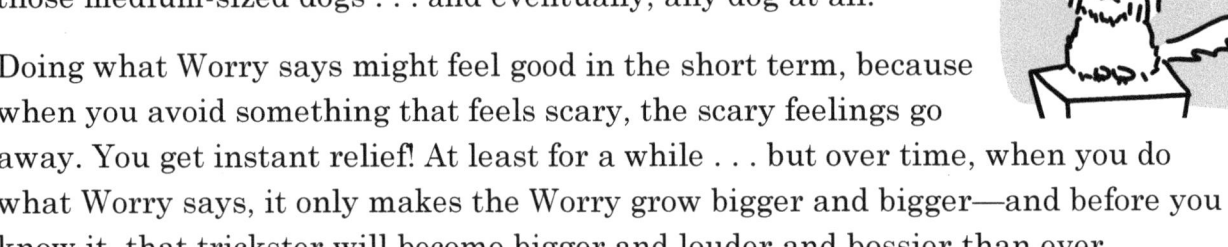

So that's the bad news. Sorry . . . ☹ But there's good news too!

We have arrived at the third big secret about Worry, and this is the most important secret of all. This is THE secret you need to know to overcome your anxiety and shrink down Worry once and for all.

Ready?

SECRET #3: BOSSING WORRY BACK WITH BRAVERY SHRINKS WORRY!

Yes, it really is that simple. **Doing the opposite of what Worry says—the brave thing—will shrink Worry over time.**

Have you ever had to deal with a bully at school trying to boss you around? Or maybe just a very demanding family member, like a brother or sister who always wants to be in charge of the game? Or maybe *you* are the oldest in your family, and sometimes you might accidentally maybe get just a *liiittle* bit bossy with your younger brother, like I used to.

Dealing with bossy people is not fun, and no one likes to be told what to do. Because of this, kids all over have already figured out how to take away a bossy person's power . . .

DON'T LISTEN TO THEM or SAY NO.

See, the thing about bossing people around is that it only works if the other person does what you say. If a kid refuses to be bossed around, the bully no longer has any power at all.

Better yet, if you get a little silly and **do the opposite** of what the bossy person is telling you . . . well, you will very quickly show the bosser who's really boss.

When I was a kid, I tried to get my younger brother Mike to follow all kinds of rules.

Do you think he listened? Of course not.

In fact, not only did he ignore my demand, but he usually went out of his way to show me that I was not in charge. If I told him to stay out, he would stop his game, walk over to my door, open it, stick his foot in, and start singing "I'm in your roo-ooom! I'm in your roo-ooom!"

How do you think I handled this? Perhaps I calmly told him that he was being quite immature?

Psssh. I threw a tantrum, of course. I'd yell at him, shriek, and tell him "Get out right now!" But he would just say "You're not the boss of me!" and keep messing around.

With Mike's expert guidance, 10-year-old me quickly learned that:

1. I am not in charge of my brother.

2. Telling my brother what to do does not work.

My brother had the right idea when he did the *opposite* of what I told him ("Don't come in my room!")—this is exactly how you want to handle Worry.

Since Worry tells you to avoid stuff, you can boss Worry back by NOT avoiding—in other words, by approaching the scary situation and trying the brave thing.

What are some of the things Worry tells you to avoid doing? Look back at which boxes you checked for the first secret and write them in the signs to the right. Then, write in what the opposite action would be.

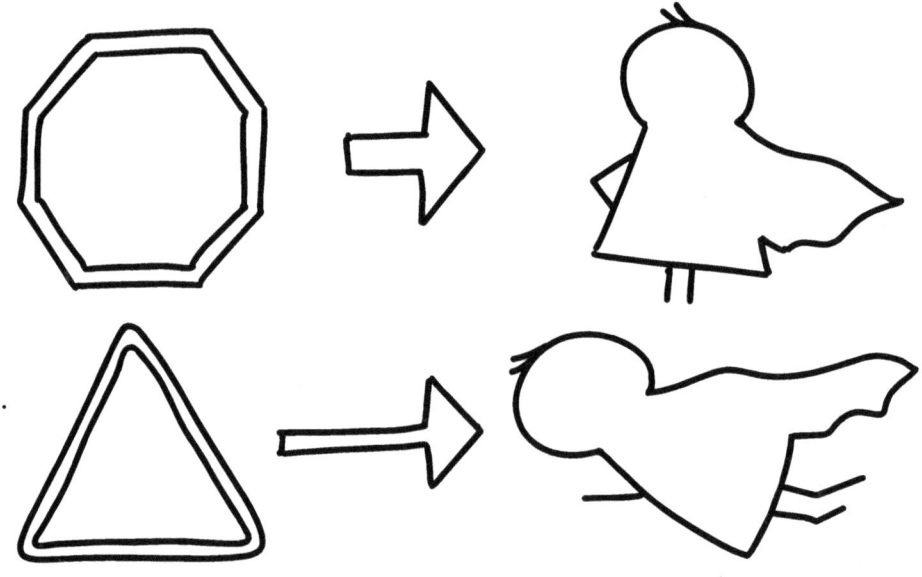

When you do the opposite of Worry—when you do the brave thing—you get to test out whether Worry is telling the truth or exaggerating how bad things will be. The more you practice, the easier it gets to catch when Worry is making something feel like a bigger deal than it really is. You quickly learn that a racing heart and sweaty palms are not a guarantee of disaster but just False Alarm Feelings that can be safely ignored.

Even better, when you practice handling those uncomfortable feelings while still doing all the stuff that matters, you learn that Worry doesn't have to stop you—you can do pretty much ANYTHING, even if anxiety is there!

This, by the way, is where **confidence** comes from. When you've bossed back Worry so much that you just *know* that you're able to handle hard stuff and try out the things that matter to you—no matter how scary, new, or unfamiliar they might be—you can stand tall and rest easy, because it's clear that *nothing* can get in your way.

So if Worry says no . . . you say YES! If Worry says "Don't go!" . . . you shrink Worry by GOING! Bossing back Worry is like a3n epic game of Reverse Simon Says. Try it out with this Boss Back Practice!

Boss Back Practice

Ask a parent or other trusted grown-up to pretend to be Worry and say the things below. Your job is to boss Worry back by saying NO and doing the opposite. (Grown-ups, a silly voice is required when playing Worry, so please channel your best Muppet impression for this task . . .)

Great job, my friend. By bossing Worry back with your actions, you have taken away its power.

Now, Worry might whine at you some more while you are challenging it, or it might try to throw a tantrum to get you to follow its commands again. How do you know if Worry is throwing a tantrum? You'll notice those False Alarm Feelings in your body get a bit bigger in the moment. That's a Worry Tantrum at work, and it's normal.

Just remember that as long as you keep doing your own thing and challenging Worry even when those uncomfortable feelings are there, the stuff you are practicing will get easier, you will get braver, and Worry will start to shrink, getting quieter and quieter. Eventually, you may shrink Worry down so far that it's easy to shrug it off and keep living your awesome life.

The Rest of This Book: Bravery-Building Dares

Now that you know all about how Worry works, it's time for US to get to work!

The rest of this book is full of bravery-building **Dares**. These are specific ways to boss back and shrink Worry through practice. Each chapter focuses on a different type of anxiety and offers its own set of Dares to help you gain confidence. These Dares will stretch you, challenge you, test your mettle . . . and hopefully be pretty fun too! You can read the chapters in order or skip around, picking only the things that Worry seems to care about for you.

Each Dare has instructions to complete the challenge, and you can use the Dare Log in appendix A to track your progress like a scientist. You can also use a feelings thermometer to keep track of how much of a tantrum Worry is having when you don't listen to its tricks.

Your mission: Try the Dare, and practice it until:

 It feels easy.

OR

 You feel confident you can handle that challenge, even if Worry shows up.

That's it!

FEELINGS THERMOMETER

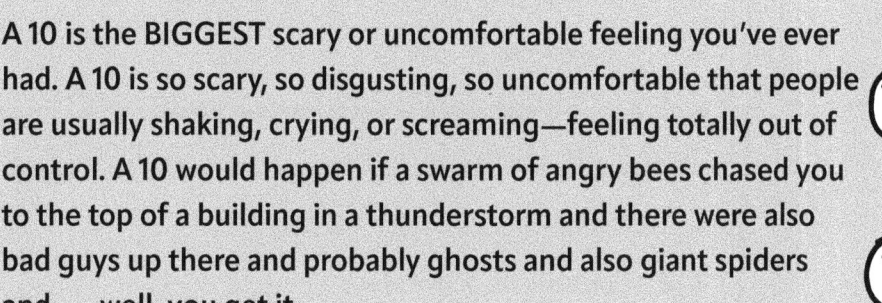

Hi! I'm a Feeling Thermometer. I take your emotional temperature and show you how big the Worry or other uncomfortable feeling is in this moment. A 0 means you don't notice the hard feeling at all. It's like you're lying on the couch and relaxing on a super chill summer day.

A 10 is the BIGGEST scary or uncomfortable feeling you've ever had. A 10 is so scary, so disgusting, so uncomfortable that people are usually shaking, crying, or screaming—feeling totally out of control. A 10 would happen if a swarm of angry bees chased you to the top of a building in a thunderstorm and there were also bad guys up there and probably ghosts and also giant spiders and... well, you get it.

Just like your body's temperature, your emotional temperature can change over time as you get more confident or comfortable, so check your temperature often! You might be surprised how fast you can go from a high temperature to a low one. Unless you're really on that rooftop with the bees and bad guys and spiders and stuff. In that case, er, good luck...

As you complete a Dare, color in the nearby *Done!* star. Or scribble the word *SUCCESS!* all over that Dare. Or heck, tear out that page, rip it up, turn it into confetti, and throw it in the air! You decide.

Once you've completed all the Dares in a chapter, you have earned the BRAVERY BADGE at the end of that chapter! Color it in, cut it out for your journal, frame it on your wall, or tape it to your forehead. You do you.

If one of the challenges in a chapter is too hard, you can make your very own series of Dares to help you work your way up to that too-tricky-for-now challenge. This is called making a *hierarchy*, or a Bravery Ladder.

Here's what a Bravery Ladder looks like:

- Give an excited big dog a treat.
- Play fetch with a big dog off leash.
- Pet a calm big dog.
- Pet a small dog that an adult is holding.
- Stand next to a calm dog on a leash.
- Stand 10 feet away from a dog on a leash.
- Stand across the street from a small dog on a leash.
- Look at a dog through a window.
- Watch a movie about dogs.
- Draw a picture of a dog.

Some Dares will have an example ladder that you can use if you want. But this is *your* Dare, so feel free to cross those things out, write in new steps on the ladder, or make an entirely new ladder that's all yours. Check out appendix B for a blank Bravery Ladder that you can copy and use for whatever your clever brain thinks up.

Some of the Dares will also list a Double Dare—a supercharged challenge for anyone who is feeling EXTRA brave that day. Other pages have an Easy Button with a suggestion for how to make the challenge easier if it feels like a bit too much (for now!). If you want to keep things casual that day, press that Easy Button and tone the challenge down. Not sure you can handle a Dare? Check out appendix C for a reminder of how awesome you are and for some ideas for making a plan that feels manageable.

Remember, these are *your* Dares to shrink *your* Worry, and you get to decide what the right amount of brave is for right now. Like a workout for your Bravery Muscles, you want the Dare to be *juuust* hard enough that it challenges you, but not so hard that it's totally overwhelming.

You can tweak any of the following to change how easy or hard a Dare is:

- Who is with you
- Where the challenge takes place
- How long the challenge is
- How far from home or your parents the challenge is
- How familiar the situation, place, or person is
- How much planning or preparation you have done
- What time of day you complete the challenge

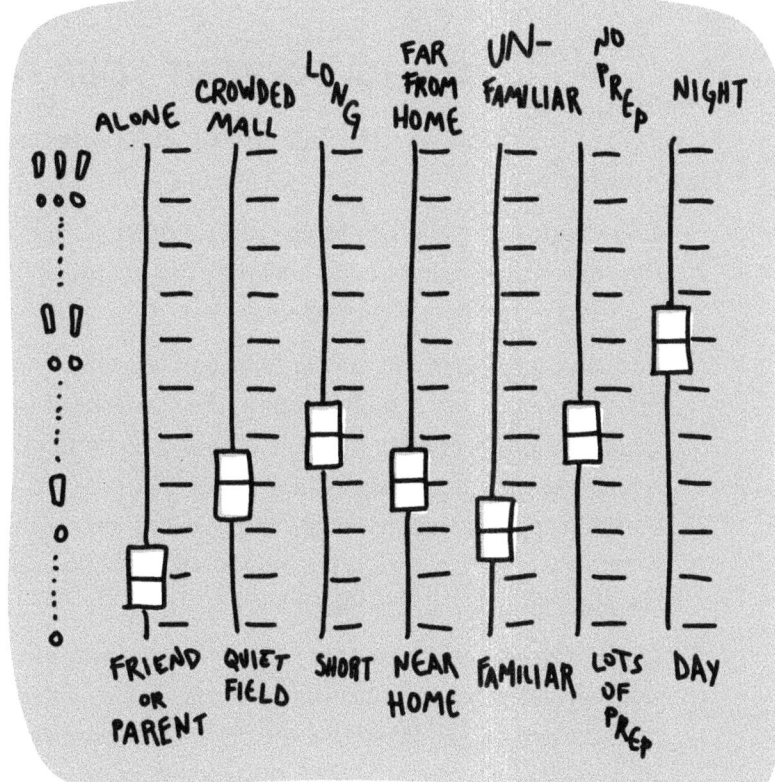

PS: Parents, counselors, and therapists make great teammates in figuring out how to tweak a Dare so that it's in the sweet spot of just-tricky-enough for you.

If you get to the end of a chapter and find yourself thinking "Wait, it's over? I'm still ready for more!" then I have good news for you: At the very end of each chapter, you'll find a few Extra Credit Dares to try. These bonus Dares are a great way to make sure that you keep the Bravery Muscles you've worked so hard to build through all your hard work. Try one whenever Worry starts to creep back and you need a Bravery Booster.

Okay, team—we are officially ready for Operation Shrink Worry. Full speed ahead!

 **HOW TO SUPPORT YOUR SOON-TO-BE BRAVER KID**

Parents play a huge role in setting kids up for success when working toward bravery. Here's how to help:

- **Coordinate opportunities for bravery:** In order for kids to make the *choice* to challenge anxiety, they need to be in situations where they can potentially choose bravery. No one goes off the high dive if they never visit a pool!

- **Remain calm:** When you remain calm, you provide a nonverbal safety signal that is much more effective than words. Children look at the reactions of their parents or other trusted adults to gauge the safety of a situation and determine whether things are okay—a process called *social referencing*. For this reason, your exterior should reflect your adult-level assessment of the risk and your child's capability. When parents, teachers, or therapists look serene and relaxed while a child is working toward facing their fears, it's often even better than if you were to shout from the rooftops "YOU CAN HANDLE THIS!"

- **Limit reassurance:** Reassurance is the secret enemy of kids with anxiety. It may seem helpful in the short term, but it actually undermines kids' confidence by treating those anxious thoughts as important and signaling that the discomfort of anxiety is so unhandleable that you need to relieve the anxiety *before* the challenge is attempted. With reassurance, you are trying to convince your child that you are *sure* it will be fine, but really, no one can know exactly how these challenges will go! Instead . . .

- **Give support:** Tell the honest truth. While you can't promise it will all be fine, you can give your child your vote of confidence. Let them know that although it might be tricky, you believe in their ability to handle the challenge, whatever might happen.

- **Reinforce success:** Celebrate bravery whenever possible, even (especially!) if the challenge was not totally smooth sailing. Facing bumps in the road is how kids gain the confidence to drive over those bumps! Play a celebration song, do a silly dance, or if you have a 6-going-on-16 kid that scoffs at parental enthusiasm, try a little smile and a quiet "nice work." If you think your kid would benefit from even more reinforcement, check out appendix D for more tips on rewarding bravery.

- **Add a teammate as necessary:** If Worry is still getting in the way after completion of these exercises, please remember that professional support can help!

CHAPTER 2
Social Stuff (Social Anxiety)

You have finally arrived at the first Dare chapter: social stuff. You might be asking yourself, "Why is social stuff the first chapter in a book about tackling anxiety? Social stuff is awesome! My favorite thing to do is hang out with my friends. What's so scary about that?"

Not so fast. Have you ever gone to a restaurant, a big party, or a brand-new almost-a-friend's house, and thought "What if I do something embarrassing? What if they think I'm boring or stupid or dumb? What if I say the wrong thing? What if I make a mistake and everyone laughs?" Have you ever had to talk in front of a class, or perform in front of others, and felt your heart start to race, your muscles get tight, and your mind go blank?

Those thoughts and feelings are the reason why this is the first chapter in this book. Please give a lukewarm welcome to our first Worry flavor: social anxiety.

What Is Social Anxiety?

Social anxiety is the fear of being judged, criticized, or rejected by others. Kids dealing with social anxiety have a carousel of "what if" questions that pop up when they meet new people, have a conversation with a classmate, or give a speech in front of others ("What if I mess up? What if everyone thinks I'm a loser?"), followed by doomsday predictions of rejection, humiliation, and ostracism.

> Ostracism involves being left out of a group. Nothing to do with ostriches. Unfortunately.

With social stuff, Worry tries to convince you that it is *essential* for everyone to approve of everything you do, all the time. If you are not 100 percent brilliant, clever, witty, and friendly in every interaction you have, Worry says you will be forever thought of as dumb, boring, and mean—making you a social outcast with no friends and no fun.

Worry gets dramatic about social stuff because a *long* time ago, back when we all lived in caves and were just figuring out this whole "fire" thing, being a part of the group was the only way to survive. We relied on our friends and family for everything. The whole group worked together to gather food, find shelter, and stay safe. Only as a group could we successfully fight off that ferocious lion lurking in the night.

This meant that long ago, being disliked by others was actually very dangerous. In those caveman times, what would happen if you were judged to be mean or dumb and then your group kicked you out? How do you think it would go if that lion saw you and thought you looked a little tasty?

The brain still responds to social risks like it did in caveman times, turning on the body's alarm system for every situation where you might be judged . . . but the thing is, we are not in caveman times anymore, and getting rejected no longer translates to getting eaten.

Worry's Tricks for Social Stuff

When it comes to social stuff, Worry will try to tell you that:

 Something very bad is going to happen in a social situation, when it's actually very unlikely.

> If you try to say hi to that group of kids at the party, they will just point and laugh at the stain on your shirt! And you'll be so upset that you'll try to run away and end up slipping on a banana peel, and then they'll laugh harder and tell the entire neighborhood, and you'll be known as "banana peel kid" for the rest of your life and . . .

16 • The Be Brave Activity Book

#2 A social mistake is a way bigger deal than it actually is.

> GASP! You messed up that kid's name at baseball practice! You mispronounced that name in front of everyone! AHHH! THIS WILL RUIN YOUR LIFE!!!

Worry likes to take it up a notch with a few bonus tricks as well:

BONUS!

NEGATIVE MIND READING: Worry tries to convince you that it can read minds—that it's able to tell you exactly what other people are thinking about you. Spoiler: It's never good.

> Uh oh. After you made that comment about the movie, Anna definitely thinks you are the most boring person on planet Earth.

BONUS!

SPOTLIGHTING: Worry tries to persuade you that there is a "spotlight" on the things you are most self-conscious about, like when you blush or have a quiver in your voice, and that everyone is paying very careful attention to that part of you.

> Look out! Every person in this room is noticing how your hands are shaking while you present . . . They all know that you are afraid. OH! And now they are noticing that you are turning red! And stumbling over your words! It's all they can focus on! Mayday! Mayday! This presentation is going DOWN!

 **WHAT ARE THE THINGS THAT WORRY SAYS TO YOU ABOUT SOCIAL STUFF?**

Worry's Social Demands

Once Worry has a grip on you, it turns bossy and starts making demands, telling you that the only way to prevent social catastrophe is to avoid any situation where others could judge you. That means . . .

- Don't share anything new about yourself
- Don't play sports
- Don't let anyone know you are anxious (hide your blushing or shaking)
- Don't ever make any social mistakes (make sure you are perfect in every interaction!)
- Don't talk to anyone new
- Don't text unless you have to
- Don't talk in a group
- Don't say anything "unscripted"
- Don't start a conversation
- Don't make that joke
- Reread any emails you write before sending
- Don't go to parties
- Plan your funny jokes and questions ahead
- Don't call people
- Don't give speeches
- Don't ask questions
- Don't share your real opinion
- Triple-check any text you send
- Don't use public bathrooms
- Don't make eye contact
- Don't wear anything unique or flashy

Mark, circle, or color in the demands that Worry has told you before. Which ones are the most annoying to you? Which ones have stopped you from doing fun stuff?

Why Avoiding Social Stuff Is a Trap

Of course, if you do avoid social stuff, you may feel safe from rejection in the short term. But in the long term, your fear of social situations only grows bigger because you never get a chance to learn whether Worry is telling the truth when it predicts that the party will go horribly or that you'll mess up big time during a presentation. You also never get to learn whether you can handle the social "hiccups" that are a totally normal part of human life, like forgetting someone's name, disagreeing with a classmate's opinion, or awkwardly pausing in a group conversation.

What's worse, when you avoid social stuff because you're worried others will judge you, it can turn into a *self-fulfilling prophecy*. That means you get so nervous about doing or saying something stupid in front of others that your social interactions actually *do* end up feeling awkward. Even worse, these awkward moments make you want to avoid social stuff even more, which is a problem, since social skills, just like other kinds of skills, take practice. If you avoid social things over and over and over, your social skills get rusty, and it gets more and more likely that there will be an awkward moment or two in your next conversation . . . which usually makes you want to avoid conversations even more.

What to Do Instead

I can't make any guarantees here, but if I were placing a bet, I would bet that you *can* handle any of the things that come up with social stuff.

UNFAMILIAR SOCIAL SITUATIONS? TOLERABLE.

UNCOMFORTABLE FEELINGS? TEMPORARY.

THE STING OF REJECTION? SURVIVABLE.

Instead of avoiding social stuff, you need to boss Worry back by . . .

1. Practicing social situations
2. Learning how to sit with the feelings that can show up when interacting with others, including cringey feelings like embarrassment (for more on "The Cringe," see chapter 10)

Just like with everything else, the more you practice, the easier it gets! So let's get to the People Party . . . on to the Dares!

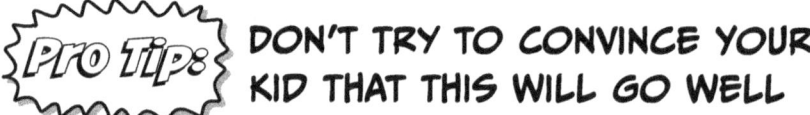

Pro Tip: DON'T TRY TO CONVINCE YOUR KID THAT THIS WILL GO WELL

For social anxiety exposures, it is doubly important that you avoid providing your child with that old reassurance fallback of "You'll be fine." That's because there are a number of factors that will contribute to the success of your child's social interaction that are totally beyond their control—namely, other living, breathing human beings.

The truth is, it may not be fine. Your child may stumble over their words in a performance. Their mind may go blank when trying to answer a question in class. The new kid they ask to play with at recess might say no. And, yes, the kids in the class might laugh and tease your child if they make a social mistake. There are no guarantees in any social situation . . . and that's okay! The goal with these Dares is to provide your child with opportunities to practice social situations, as well as to practice tolerating all of the feelings and follies that can show up during that unpredictable verbal dance we call "conversation."

Success is not about having a social interaction go perfectly. Success is about having your child try social stuff and learn that even when a social situation goes badly, it is not the world-ending catastrophe that Worry predicted it to be—*and* those uncomfortable thoughts and feelings don't have to stop them from doing what matters.

Social Stuff: Dares

ASK WHAT TIME IT IS

Who wears a watch these days? Not you! Or maybe you. But today we're going to pretend you don't. Walk up to a person you don't know and ask what time it is! Try making eye contact when asking and smiling when you say thanks.

 **Play Time Teller Bingo!**
Try this challenge out in different places with different people. How many boxes can you fill on the grid below?

	In a restaurant	In a store	At school
Ask an adult			
Ask another kid			
Ask an employee			

Chapter 2 • Social Stuff (Social Anxiety) • 21

 HAVE A QUESTION-FREE CONVERSATION

Everyone knows the easiest way to keep a conversation going is to ask questions.

However, if you've been on the receiving end of those endless questions, you know that the interaction can quickly switch from "conversation" to "interview."

Today, try the opposite: See if you can have a three-minute conversation with someone where you ask them no questions at all!

When you're feeling stuck, instead of asking a question, try *self-disclosure*. That's when you share something about yourself that is related to the person you are talking to or the topic of conversation. Self-disclosure can feel a little spooky at first. (Worry will tell you that you're sharing something about yourself that could be criticized!) But remember that sharing your thoughts and opinions is exactly how you start to feel closer to others and develop friendships . . . so disclose away!

Bill: Hi, Bob!

Bob: Hi, Bill! I was just thinking about those cookies you made for the team, they were so delicious! I want to try that recipe sometime.

Bill: Oh, I'll have to send it you! I've been making more cakes recently, though.

Bob: I love cakes! Chocolate is my favorite.

Bill: My preferred cake is a pickle and ice cream cake, if I'm being honest.

Bob: Uh . . . wow . . . sounds delicious . . .

22 • The Be Brave Activity Book

DARE 3: BE ASSERTIVE

Channel your inner Boss today by being assertive in a group! *Assertiveness* means being honest and direct with others when you talk to them. Kids who are assertive share their true opinions and feelings even when it's a little uncomfortable to do so. Assertiveness is one tool that kids and adults can use to build confidence.

BEING ASSERTIVE COULD BE:
- Saying no if you are asked to do something you don't want to do
- Sharing your real opinion, even if it is not the same as the group's opinion
- Asking for things you want or need
- Offering your own ideas or suggestions
- Politely disagreeing in a way that respects others' opinions
- Speaking up for someone else

BEING ASSERTIVE LOOKS LIKE:
- Making eye contact
- Standing tall
- Acting calm
- Using a "just loud enough" voice
- Stating your beliefs clearly

When deciding what to be assertive about, feel free to pick a topic that's a Great Big Deal to you, or a topic that's not so serious. Maybe you have strong feelings about who should be the pitcher for your baseball team or about the correct way to assemble a peanut butter and jelly sandwich. Maybe you strongly believe that bullying is NEVER EVER acceptable. Or maybe you think Taylor Swift's new album is (*gasp*) only okay.

No matter what topic you pick, take a moment to stand up straight before you start talking, take a deep breath, and make eye contact. Then go for it! Let everyone know how you really feel. You might just find that others feel the same!

 ASK FOR AN OPINION

Worry wants you to avoid doing or saying anything that could cause you to be judged by other kids, and that means that asking for opinions is off the table. If someone gives you their opinion, it might mean (eeek!) disagreement. Let's test that out and see how disagreeable everyone really is, AND whether disagreeing is a big deal or a little one . . .

Ask for an opinion from someone your age after sharing your own thoughts. You might ask:

- What do you think of this shirt? I kind of like the color.
- How did you feel about that new movie? I thought it was hilarious.
- Which book should I check out? I'm thinking something fantasy . . .
- I'm such a fan of brussels sprouts! Do you like them?

DOUBLE DARE

Instead of just asking for an opinion, ask for a critique! Try these on for size:
- What would you change about my ____?
- Is there anything I should do to improve on ____?
- What can I do differently next time for ____?

FEEDBACK PLEASE!

24 • The Be Brave Activity Book

DARE 5: COMPLIMENT SOMEONE

Crush everyone with kindness today—compliment five people you don't know well!

Consider these options:

- Love the new song, Wolfgang!
- Super fun outfit, Miley!
- That was a really impressive serve, Serena!
- I appreciate the way you handled that Death Eater, Harry!
- Why, Grandmother, what big teeth you have!

Word of advice: Do not pick the last one. Does not end well.

Compliments have a special kind of magic to them because the good feelings go both ways: Getting a compliment makes a person feel good about themselves, and it's a pretty cool feeling to know you've brightened someone's day too!

DARE 6: DIGITALLY CONNECT WITH NEW-ISH FRIENDS

Usually wait for someone else to start the conversation? Be the first to reach out today—text, call, or message three new-ish acquaintances or friends. You can send a picture or GIF, text a homework question, say good morning or goodnight, check how their day is going, or call and ask what their deepest, darkest secret is. Whatever you do, try to pick people you like that you think would be one step outside your comfort zone—*juuust* intimidating enough that reaching out first feels tricky.

Person 1: _____

Person 2: _____

Person 3: _____

DARE 7: PARTY TIME

Let the good times roll—this Dare challenges you to find some PARTY TIME!

There are three ways to get yourself to a party:

- Go to a party you are invited to.
- Go to a party you are not invited to (Note: not recommended).
- *Be* the party: Host a gathering.

Your party can be anywhere from 3 to 300 people, as long as it's a get-together that is special for some reason. Check out www.nationaltoday.com to find a reason to celebrate. National Grilled Cheese Sandwich Day, here we come!

Remember, parties are a part of life where you can't control everything. Sometimes the music isn't your style, the food is new to you, or there are people there who you don't know. Someone unfamiliar might ask a question you don't know the answer to. This is okay! Let's test how handleable those "surprise" parts of a party are.

EVERY PARTY IS A SURPRISE PARTY

Even when you are the host of a party, surprising or unexpected things can still happen. Two of your friends might get into an argument, the chicken wings may be delivered later than you planned, or someone could secretly fill your hall closet with balloons. (Not gonna lie, I hope this last one happens to you.) Not everyone will like everything about the party either. There is no one song or food that Every. Single. Person. Loves. That's okay, because the goal is not to throw the perfect party . . . it's to get more confident about your ability *to* party and to handle all the stuff that goes with it!

 ## PLAY A GROUP GAME

Worry says group games are risky. By playing on a team, whether it be charades or frisbee or soccer or bowling, there's a chance you won't perform well and might let the team down. Worry will tell you that this is unacceptable—that your teammates will think badly of you and that you will *never* recover.

But Worry doesn't want you to take note of one important fact: *Everyone* makes mistakes sometimes, and everyone also *knows* that everyone makes mistakes sometimes. This is why when you see a goalie jump the wrong way and let a goal slip by, teammates will walk over and pat the goalie on the back, and then get right back to playing.

Practice being a teammate and play a game with a group! Challenge yourself by:

- Picking a game that you don't know perfectly well

    OR

- Playing a game with some people you don't know very well

If unfamiliar group games or new people feel extra tricky, check out the sample Bravery Ladder below for ideas on how to work up to all that group goodness.

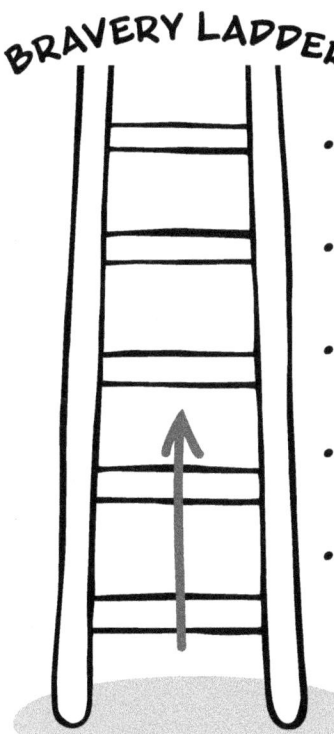

- Play a group game that is new to you, with people you don't know well.
- Play a group game you have played before, with people you don't know well.
- Play a group game that is new to you, with people you know.
- Play a group game that you know you are good at, with people you know.
- Watch a group game and "tag in" for a few minutes if someone needs a break.

 ## DARE 9 — ASK A STRANGER FOR DIRECTIONS

Make sure you know where you're going and what you are doing in this wild, wild world—ask a stranger for directions!

You can request information on how to get to the toy section at Target, how to get to a restaurant three blocks over, how to place an online order, or how to achieve world domination . . . your call.

 ## DARE 10 — MAKE A NEW FRIEND

Take a step in the bestie direction and invite someone new to hang out today.

We all have those people who fall into the category of "Friend Candidate." That's someone who you think is nice, seems friendly, and shares an interest with you—a deep love of cheese curds, perhaps.

Invite that Friend Candidate to come over for video games after school, to study in the library over lunch, or to go anywhere else, for any other reason. You could hang out inside or outside, at the mall, at the playground, at the park, at school, or at home—your house or theirs. What matters is that you spend time with someone new-ish who you would like to know better.

SOCIAL BRAVERY BADGE

Check all those DONE! boxes?

CONGRATULATIONS! You have earned your **Social Bravery Badge**.

EXTRA CREDIT

Still want more? Try out a few Extra Credit Dares below:

▷ Go to a coffee shop and order something not on the menu.

▷ Plan and host a virtual hangout.

▷ Say yes to any and all invitations for a week.

▷ Go on a social scavenger hunt: collect five moments of eye contact, four smiles, three hellos, two short conversations, and one long conversation.

▷ Poll 10 strangers about their favorite ice cream flavor.

CHAPTER 3
School Stuff (School Anxiety)

Recently, the world has come up with a new phrase to describe that uncomfortable oh-no feeling of dread that shows up right before the school week starts: the Sunday Scaries. It's that feeling you get toward the end of the weekend when you start to realize that the break is over and you have a whole WEEK of school ahead of you, full of homework and classmates and fire drills and gym class and tests and answering questions and who-knows-what-else . . . yeah. That feeling.

The Sunday Scaries is a common feeling that kids *and* adults experience if they know they have a hard week ahead, and the feeling usually goes away once the weekday gets started. But kids wrestling with Worry sometimes have a supersized version of the Sunday Scaries that shows up not just on Sunday, but on Monday and Tuesday and Wednesday and Thursday too. For these kids, school doesn't just feel hard, it feels TERRIFYING . . .

What Is School Anxiety?

School anxiety involves a fear of one or more specific experiences that happen at school. Some school things that Worry might be chattering about include:

- Riding the bus
- Giving a presentation
- Taking a test
- Getting called on in class
- Fire/tornado/lockdown drills
- Working in a group

- Separating from your parents
- Getting teased about your clothing
- Making a mistake in front of the class
- Playing on a team in gym class
- Eating in the lunchroom
- Using the school bathrooms
- Needing to visit the nurse when sick
- Someone throwing up nearby
- Going on field trips
- Something totally different that's not even on this list

Kind of a long list, right?! Does Worry bother you about any of this stuff? Circle the ones on the list that Worry gets loud about.

Now for some good news: School is actually an incredible bravery builder because it challenges you to take small steps outside your comfort zone every day. Each week, you are asked to learn something new, try activities you may not know how to do just yet, perform in front of others, and spend time with kids and adults you may or may not know very well. School is eight hours a day of get-used-to-it practice for social interaction, mistakes, performance, and not knowing stuff! This means that if you find a way to boss Worry back and get brave about school, you will automatically get braver about all that other stuff too. I love a two-for-one deal, don't you?

Worry's Tricks for School Stuff

In order for us to work together on this type of anxiety, we'll need some more intel on what specific things Worry says about school. Here is where Worry's tricks get a bit more academic (duh). Worry will try to tell you that:

  Something very bad is going to happen at school, when it's actually very unlikely.

The school bus will break down on the way to pick you up from school! And then the bus driver will have to call a mechanic and forget to tell the school that the bus is broken because he's hungry and sees a hot dog stand, and then NO ONE will come to pick you up! And then you'll be stuck at school forever and ever, and your family will set off on a life without you, and you'll be stuck working as the school janitor, and . . .

#2 An academic or performance mistake is a way bigger deal than it actually is.

GASP! You stumbled over that word in your speech! Everyone heard it! And the teacher did too, so now you can't possibly get a good grade! THIS IS THE DESTRUCTION OF EVERYTHING!

#3 If the bad thing happens at school, you will never recover, when the reality is you can definitely bounce back and move on.

If you fail the math test, your academic life is RUINED! Your disappointment and shame will be INFINITE AND NEVER-ENDING! You will lose all confidence in the ability to multiply anything, your grades will never recover, and you'll have to drop out of school and work in coal mines or something. RIP career.

WHAT ARE THE TRICKY THINGS THAT WORRY SAYS TO YOU ABOUT SCHOOL STUFF?

Worry's School Demands

These tricks are followed by an avalanche of "don't" demands where Worry insists that you avoid school stuff. Look at each of the categories below and write down or draw the things that Worry tells you NOT to do at school:

GETTING TO AND FROM SCHOOL
"Don't get on the bus! Don't separate from your parents! Don't go!"

SPECIALS (GYM, MUSIC, ETC.)
"Don't run too much! Don't participate!"

CLASS TIME
"Don't raise your hand!"

TIME WITH FRIENDS
"Don't tell that joke! Don't share your opinion!"

RECESS
"Don't play that game with the group!"

PRESENTATIONS OR TESTS
"Don't present in front of the class!"

LUNCH
"Don't eat in front of others!"

Chapter 3 • **School Stuff (School Anxiety)** • 33

Why Avoiding School Stuff Is a Trap

Here's the thing: Everything Worry is telling you to do boils down to one command. Connect the dots to find out what it is . . .

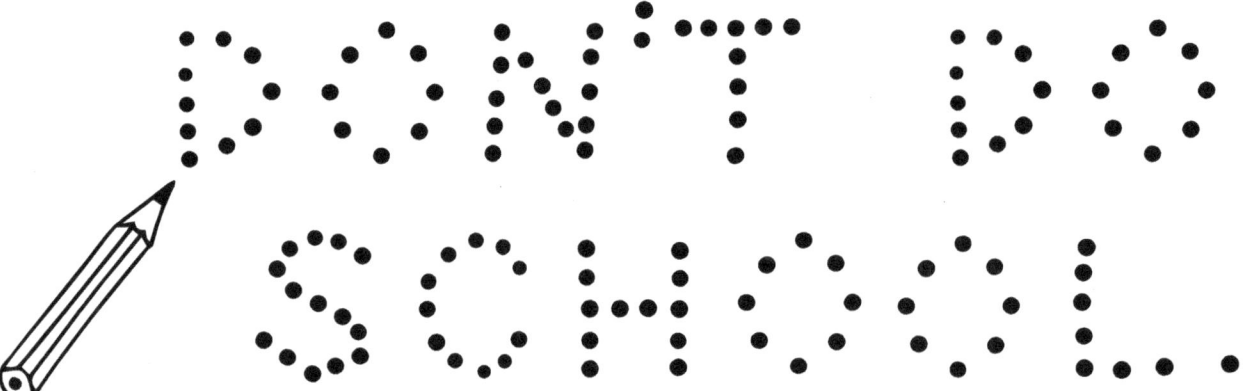

DON'T DO SCHOOL.

However, there are three big problems with listening to Worry and never attending school again:

 SOME VERSION OF SCHOOL IS OFFICIALLY REQUIRED FOR KIDS. EVERYWHERE.

Grown-ups don't let this one slide. School is required for kids and teens. It's required by parents, communities, and state and federal law—by basically everyone, pretty much everywhere. This is because . . .

 DOING SCHOOL IS IMPORTANT FOR MANY OF THE THINGS THAT YOU WANT TO DO IN LIFE.

Want to be an astronaut? Definitely need school for that. Want to play college basketball and see your face on ESPN? You'll need to get accepted into a college first, and that means school. Want to get a job and earn oodles of money and buy a mansion with a swimming pool, a gold statue of your poodle, and eight fancy cars? Or at least have a job that earns enough money so you don't have to live in your parents' basement forever? School will make that about a million times easier.

AND MOST IMPORTANTLY . . .

#3 AVOIDING SCHOOL MAY FEEL GOOD IN THE SHORT TERM, BUT DOING SO WILL MAKE YOU LESS AND LESS CONFIDENT OVER TIME.

School is basically eight hours of life-in-the-real-world training. It's learning how to handle frustration and boredom (I'm looking at you, Least Favorite Class). It's practice working together with people who might not always agree with you and balancing different commitments and expectations. It's learning how to present and share your ideas in front of others—a must if you want to start a business, influence a group, or just, you know, change the world. It's figuring out how to move forward even when a task gets hard.

Every time you practice even one of these things, you get a little more confident because you prove to yourself that you *can* handle that uncomfortable or tricky school situation! However, every time you avoid school, you are telling yourself the opposite: "I can't cope with that." Plus, you never get the chance to see if your anxious thought is true. Worry wins by default when you don't try.

What to Do Instead

Your goal is to show Worry that even if school feels uncomfortable—even if you don't know exactly how the school day will go—you are willing to give school a try by practicing all those situations that Worry seems to care so much about. That means raising your hand in class, getting in on that game of dodgeball, volunteering to give that class presentation, and being open to whatever other school adventures come your way.

Remember, the more you practice, the easier it gets . . .

NOW ON TO THE DARES!

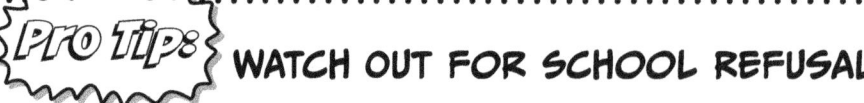
WATCH OUT FOR SCHOOL REFUSAL

Sometimes school anxiety gets big enough that kids start telling their parents—usually very loudly—that they are NOT going to school. This is called *school refusal*, and it's pretty common when school worries are present.

If you've got a kid in this camp, fear not. Anxiety-driven school refusal is manageable and often reduced or eliminated as soon as kids build up the confidence that they can handle the school situation. The Dares that follow will help build this confidence.

Of course, the only way to do any kind of school Dare practice is to get kids in the (school) door. That means the main goal in tackling anxiety-based school refusal is *attendance*. A child's physical presence at school, as much as possible, is key—increasing over time if necessary.

If you are struggling to get your kid in those school doors, check out the School Refusal Playbook in appendix E. It has more specific directions for getting your kid to say yes to school, even if they are not (yet!) feeling totally brave.

School Stuff: Dares

DARE 11: GIVE A PRESENTATION

You can move one step closer to all those press conferences you'll be giving as a famous singer, professional athlete, or president by polishing your public speaking skills. How? Give a presentation in front of others at school!

Lots of people find it hard to share their ideas in front of others. Public speaking is the most common fear there is, even more common than the fear of death. And if talking in front of random people is hard, then talking in front of classmates can be . . . yikes. For this Dare, select your preferred level of bravery: If the idea of a full-class presentation is too hard for now, check out the Bravery Ladder on the next page and pick the presentation level that's Goldilocks-style just-hard-enough.

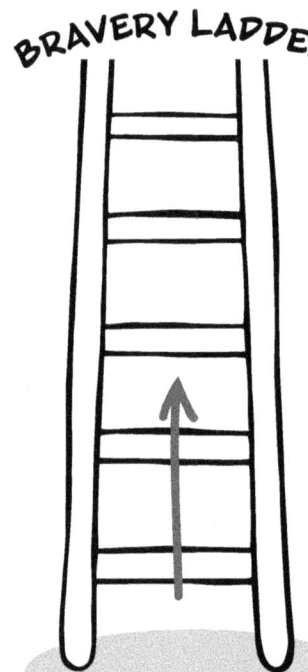

BRAVERY LADDER

- Present for 5–10 minutes in front of your full class.
- Present for 3 minutes in front of your full class.
- Present for 2–5 minutes in front of a club or team.
- Present for 3 minutes in front of two classmates.
- Present for 2 minutes in front of a single teacher.

Some topics to present on could be:

- What you did this summer
- What you are doing during winter break

- Something you want your class to know about you
- A topic that's important to you

- Your family traditions
- An interesting animal
- A culture's traditions

 Split the work and present with a friend!

 ## ASK A QUESTION IN CLASS

How many times have you had a question that popped into your mind when a teacher was talking? Only about a million times? And how many of those questions got asked out loud to your teacher? If you are like most kids, the answer is . . . well, not a million of them.

Banish IDK from your day today and give your arm a workout by raising your hand and asking questions in three classes.

In the space below, list the classes or subjects you will ask your questions in:

Here are some general questions to get you started:
- Can you please explain that last part again?
- What does _____ mean?
- When is this homework due?
- Will this topic be on the test next week?

 ## DARE 13 WEAR SOMETHING FLASHY TO SCHOOL

Worry can try to tell you that anything attention-grabbing is a bad idea. What if other kids think your new shoes look funny? What if they judge you to be unstylish? You could never handle that! Just kidding. Of course you can.

To boss Worry back, let's get FANCY! Bright colors! Bold prints! Ball gowns! Well, for school, maybe just the first two . . .

In fashion, you can never please everyone, but you can please yourself. Today is the day to try that pair of neon green zebra print leggings you have yet to wear, or those amazing new metallic gold sneakers you asked for on your birthday. It's the day to wear the piece of clothing in your closet that you love but that makes you just a tiny bit uncomfortable. Let's see just how many people notice that extra spice in your wardrobe—and whether they like it too!

 ## DARE 14 ANSWER A QUESTION IN CLASS

Put on your smarty pants today, let that brain shine, and raise your hand to answer a question in class! Boss Worry a little extra by turning the volume up on your voice a few notches when you give your answer so it's loud and clear.

EASY BUTTON: Pick a question to answer where you are very confident in your answer.

DOUBLE DARE: Answer a hard question with your best guess. It might be wrong, but you can handle wrong!

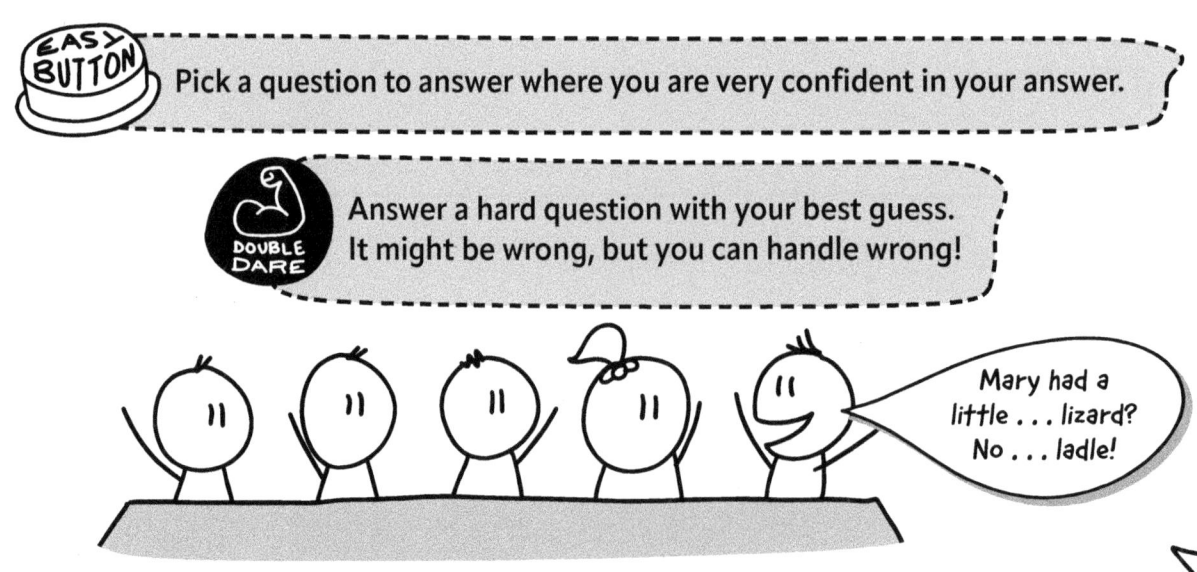

DARE 15: EXPLORE AN INTEREST

Make time for fun and maybe even make some new friends with this Dare: Attend a school club meeting that you have never attended before. Check with your teacher about when and where the next meeting is, and arrive a few minutes early to meet the teacher or staff person that leads the group.

Every school has a different menu of options for sports and activity clubs, but a few options to get you started might be:

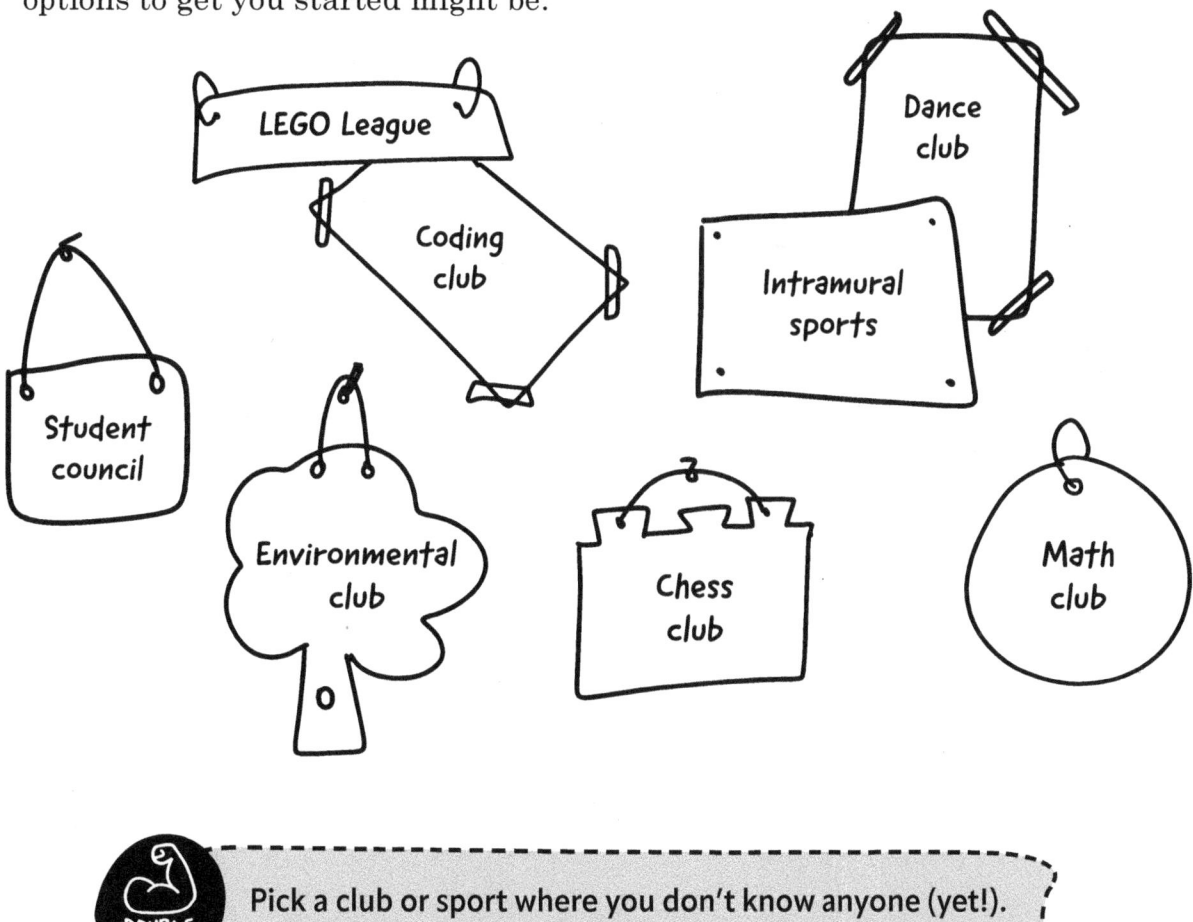

DOUBLE DARE: Pick a club or sport where you don't know anyone (yet!).

 ## MEET WITH A TEACHER FOR HELP

Make the trickiest subject just a little less tricky today: Meet one-on-one with a teacher to get help with a difficult subject.

Worry always tells you to avoid the most uncomfortable or confusing school subjects, and certainly to avoid asking for help. Worry might be saying . . .

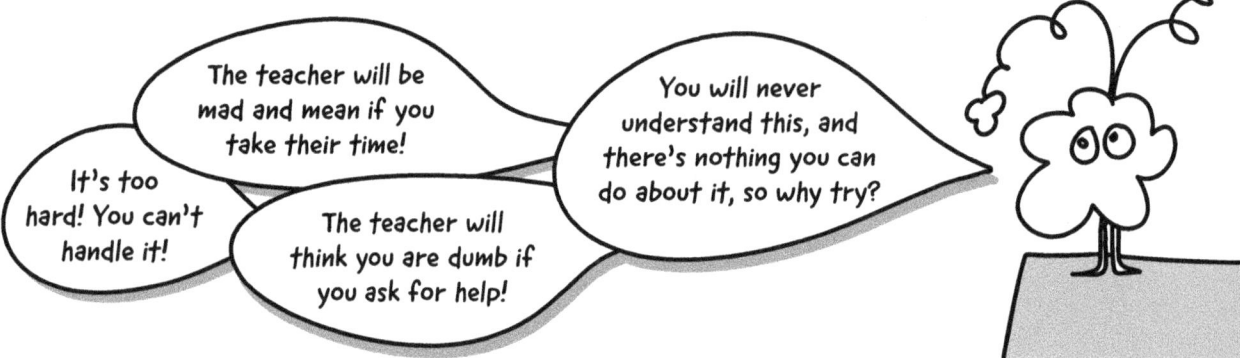

Let's call Worry's bluff and see if any of that is true. Ask your teacher for a chance to meet before school, during lunch, or after school for little extra explanation on that tricky topic.

 ## HANG WITH SOMEONE NEW AT LUNCH

Ah, lunchtime. Finally, a break where you can relax, have a snack or five, and do what you do best: hang with friends.

For this lunch period, expand those friend horizons: Sit and talk with someone new at the lunch table. You can pick anyone, but for maximum bravery impact, select someone who's a Friend Candidate—someone you think is nice, friendly, and might share an interest. (See Dare 10 in chapter 2 for more information on Friend Candidates.)

42 • The Be Brave Activity Book

 ## DARE 18 — START A CONVERSATION WITH A CLASSMATE

Be the chatterbox you know you can be today by starting a conversation with a classmate. For this Dare, pick someone who's not already a close friend—someone you don't talk to every day. To get the ball rolling with your unsuspecting conversation partner, try one of the following:

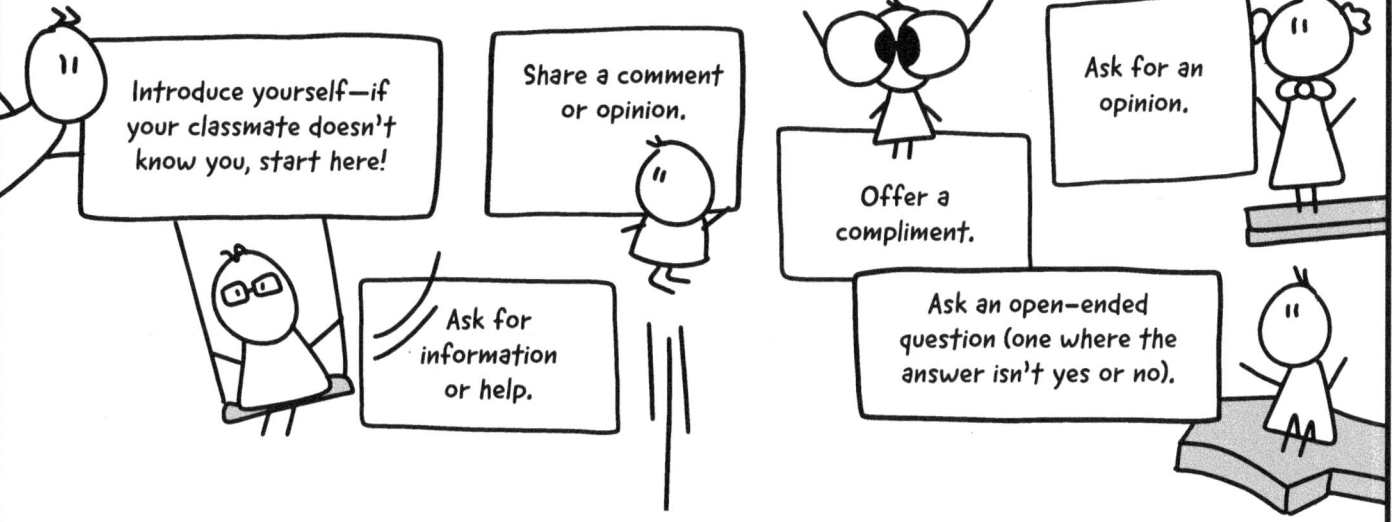

- Introduce yourself—if your classmate doesn't know you, start here!
- Ask for information or help.
- Share a comment or opinion.
- Offer a compliment.
- Ask for an opinion.
- Ask an open-ended question (one where the answer isn't yes or no).

Remember to turn on your **LISTENING EARS** for their response and to show interest by looking at the person and reacting to their reply with a smile, nod, or comment of your own!

 ## DARE 19 — 3 BY 3S

Shoot out a few extra beams of friendliness today with a set of what I call 3 by 3s: Make eye contact, smile, and say hi to three classmates. Log the people you choose, check that you did all three, and see how they respond!

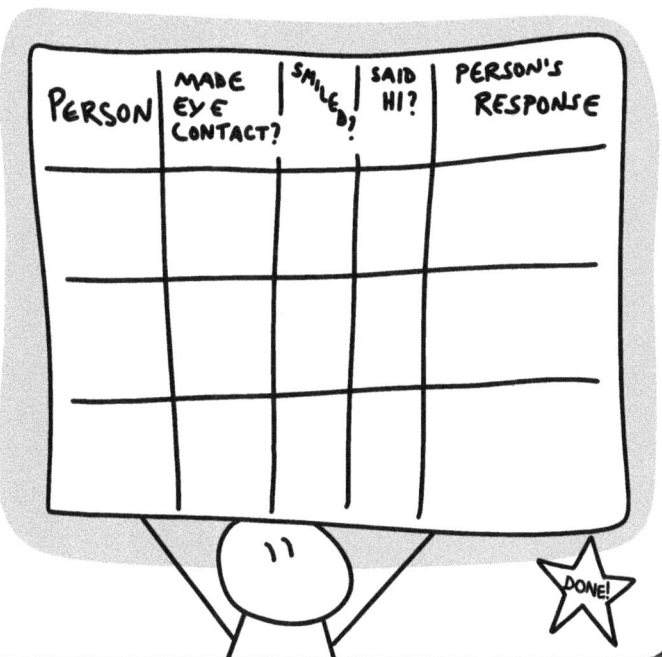

Person	Made eye contact?	Smiled?	Said hi?	Person's response

Chapter 3 • School Stuff (School Anxiety) • 43

 ## JOIN A GROUP CONVERSATION

Practice saddling up to social situations with the final Dare of this chapter: Join a group conversation. Pick a group standing in a loose semi-circle. (You don't want the circle to be tight, as that can mean the conversation is private.) Drift over to the group and start listening. Feel free to add a "Hi, everyone!" or a little smile and wave if people turn toward you. When you have an idea of what's going on, chime in with a thought or opinion.

Before you join the crowd, here are a few key pieces of advice for easy group entry and smooth social sailing:

- If you don't know anyone in the group, like at a new club meeting, introduce yourself first.

- When joining a group at a lunch table, asking "Is it okay if I sit here?" can get you instant group membership after someone says "Sure!"

- Ask a question about the conversation topic ("Are we talking about everyone's favorite vacuum cleaner right now?"), or about something you have in common with the group ("Ugh, Mrs. Ultrateacher's science homework is so intense, right?"). This can be a casual way to start talking.

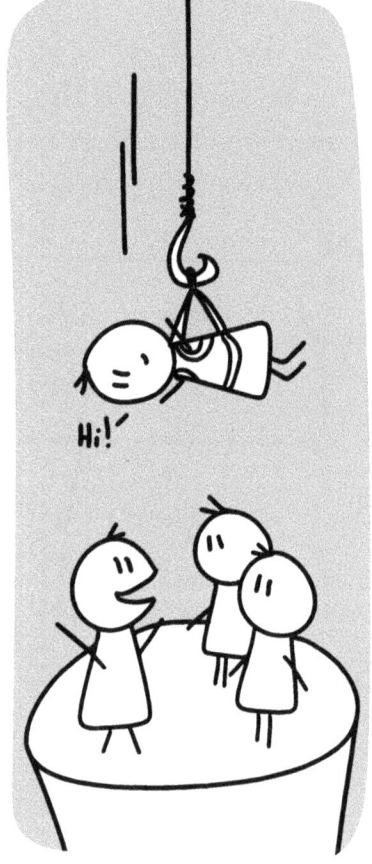

SCHOOL BRAVERY BADGE

Check all those ⭐ boxes?

CONGRATULATIONS! You have earned your **School Bravery Badge**.

EXTRA CREDIT

Still want more? Try out a few Extra Credit Dares below:

➡ Bring something messy to eat in the lunchroom.

➡ Email a question to a teacher or coach.

➡ Try hard in gym class.

➡ Ask to use the bathroom during class.

➡ Ask a question in the main office.

CHAPTER 4
Doing Stuff Alone
(Separation Anxiety)

When you're a year old, the most thrilling thing in the world is taking that first wobbly step out of your parents' arms and into the great beyond—beyond Mom's reach, that is. Toddlers savor the ability to tell their parents, NO STAY AWAY, that they will be doing it THEMSELVES, thank you very much (even if "doing it themselves" takes about four times as long and makes a giant mess).

Independence is a celebrated part of getting older—whether it's your first time sleeping over at a friend's house, or you pass your driving test and take the car for your first solo spin—and all those exciting firsts give you a delicious taste of sweet, sweet freedom. However, that taste of freedom can quickly turn from sweet to sour when Worry tries to take charge.

What Is Separation Anxiety?

Separation anxiety occurs when kids feel nervous or scared anytime they are separated from the grown-ups who usually take care of them. These kids stress not only about their ability to do things on their own, but also about the safety of themselves and their parents. With separation anxiety, it feels like something terrible will happen if you don't have instant access to the adults you know you can count on to keep you safe.

Now, pretty much all kids struggle with separation some of the time—it can be hard to say goodbye to someone you love, even for a short while! But when Worry sinks its teeth in, it starts to feel almost *impossible* for you to separate, and when you do, it feels like "Goodbye for now" is actually "Goodbye forever."

Worry's Tricks for Separation

What is Worry telling you about separation? A bunch of separation-flavored Worry tricks, of course! Worry will try to tell you that:

#1) If you separate from your dad/mom/grandma/big brother/Great-Aunt Sally, something AWFUL will happen to you or to them . . . even though the awful thing is incredibly unlikely.

If you walk away from Dad to go pick apples at this farm, you will be kidnapped by one of those evil kidnappers! YES, they DO lurk in apple orchards! They will sneak up behind you and put an apple bucket over your head and scoop you up and drive away with the hayride tractor, and Dad will never know!

Worry's Separation Demands

No matter what separation tricks Worry is using on you, it is almost always making the same demand:

DO NOT UNDER ANY CIRCUMSTANCES SEPARATE FROM YOUR ADULT!

Color in all the situations below where Worry says you should never let your adults out of sight:

Why Never Separating Is a Bad Idea

If Worry had its way, you would be glued to your parent or other safe adult 24-7-365, and in some ways, this might feel nice. You love your grown-up after all, and the feelings that show up with separation are uncomfortable! Sadness, homesickness, that "missing you" feeling . . . those are definitely unpleasant emotions to experience. And Worry's not wrong: If a parent goes away on an overnight trip, or even on an errand around the block, you can't be 100 percent SURE that nothing bad will happen.

BUT IF YOU NEVER SEPARATE FROM YOUR PARENTS, YOU ALSO NEVER GET THE CHANCE TO:

- Go with friends to the park
- Go on field trips with your class
- Have a sleepover with a friend
- Drive a car by yourself
- Go to college
- Get a job
- Have any alone time ever

What are the ways in which life might be more fun if separating was easy?

DRAW YOUR OWN IDEAS HERE.

"I'd go to my friend's house and fill her bathtub with bubbles and floaties and ten pounds of glitter for the fanciest pool party ever, and no one would stop me!"

"Well, your friend might have something to say about that..."

What to Do Instead

If Worry keeps telling you "Don't separate!" then you need to practice doing the opposite. That means making today and every other day INDEPENDENCE DAY! Each step away from your parents is a step toward a more confident you, and that's something worth celebrating.

Now, channel your inner two-year-old and tell your parents "I do it by MYSELF" with the Dares that follow. No tantrums required.

"Um seriously, please, no tantrums... pretty please?"

Chapter 4 • Doing Stuff Alone (Separation Anxiety) • 51

 **GO FROM GLUE TO RUBBER WITH THE BRAVE GOODBYE**

When dealing with separation anxiety, parents often find themselves with a monkey on their back. This monkey is not metaphorical but literal: In anxiety-provoking situations, your own little primate suddenly turns into a stage-five clinger, physically attaching themselves to you in any situation where separation is a possibility. These kiddos often require a direct, manual transfer to another adult, such as a teacher, in separation situations like kindergarten drop-off, and it's not always pretty.

Barnacle behavior is not terribly surprising when separation is spooky. If Worry tells your child that the only way to stay safe is to *not* separate from you, well, your kid may interpret that in a literal (a.k.a. physical) way. When close feels safe, closer feels safer. And let's not forget, snuggles with a calm parent are one way that kids—especially the littlest ones who are five and under—can calm their bodies, an adaptive process referred to as *co-regulation*.

However, when a child clings to their parent in *every* uncomfortable moment, it does not serve them well, especially before separation. That's because our body language and posture actually impact our neurobiology, and when a child is clinging to their grown-up with that crunched, anxious posture, it signals to their brain that the situation is dangerous and unmanageable (even when it's not!). In other words, when a kid cowers behind their parent like Scooby-Doo does with Shaggy, it leaves that kid *feeling* like Scooby when they're faced with the prospect of going somewhere alone.

To manage this, you need to get out the spatula, scrape your kids off your legs, and practice confident separation with the Brave Goodbye. Here's what a Brave Goodbye looks like:

The Before: Brave Body
Channel your inner superhero, your favorite celebrity, or the most confident person you know and borrow their posture. Stand tall, with your shoulders back, your arms uncrossed, and your hands at your sides (or tucked in your pockets or on your hips). This is called *Brave Body*, and it will help everyone—kids and adults alike—feel more confident during a separation.

The Goodbye: One and Done
Give a single goodbye and make it count! Give one big hug (or a high five if hugs start to turn sticky) followed by a calm "Goodbye, I love you!" Keep it consistent, every time. Short and sweet is best, with a little silly humor sprinkled in if desired. A "Catch you later, alligator" or "Gotta go, buffalo"—followed by your child's "See you soon, big baboon"—may even give you a shot at a goodbye that includes giggles.

The After: Turn and Burn
Last, turn toward your destination and walk away with purpose using Brave Body. No peeking back to see if your child is still waving goodbye, no quick curtain call hug, and no encore goodbye. Keep moving!

Final note: One of the ways you help your child feel confident that separation is safe is by modeling it yourself. Therefore, make sure to channel that relaxed and confident posture, and stick to a single goodbye paired with a quick getaway. Plus, by limiting how long a drop-off takes, you also are likely to limit how long your child is in distress-signaling mode versus re-regulating mode.

A Brave Goodbye can be paired and practiced with most of the Dares that follow. Introduce your child to the sequence ahead of time and practice in the house when no separation is planned. If you go through the new routine 5 to 10 times on Saturday morning, your child won't be blindsided by the change come Monday's school drop-off.

Separation: Dares

DARE 21: BE KING OF THE CASTLE

The next time you're at home, pretend that your house is *all* yours.

And I don't mean that you just live there with your parents as roomies. Take a page from Kevin McCallister in that classic movie *Home Alone* and pretend that it's *your* house—yours and yours alone. Spend one hour as King of the Castle in a different part of your house, away from your parents. Banish your parents to the basement (ahem, dungeon?), garage, patio, or some other part of the house or yard where you can't see them.

It is good to be King, but it comes with responsibility too. For this whole hour, plan on getting your own snacks, refilling your own water, and bossing back your own Worry when it shows up. You got this!

DARE 22: SEND YOUR PARENTS ON AN ERRAND

Practice handling life parent-free by sending one or both of your grown-ups out on an errand. If staying home alone is not an option yet, this Dare might need to involve one parent at a time, or it might mean inviting an aunt, uncle, neighbor, or family friend to tag in and keep an eye on things.

Work with your parents to pick an errand, plan who will be with you (if needed), and figure out how long the errand will take. Will this be a 10-minutes-at-the-corner-store visit? A 2-hour Target run? Or an all-evening date night? Pick an errand length and location that feels like it might be one step outside your comfort zone. Check out the sample Bravery Ladder below for ideas.

BRAVERY LADDER

I stay home while . . .

- Both parents go to a movie in the evening and don't respond to check-in texts.
- Both parents run errands for two hours and will reply to one check-in text.
- Mom goes to the library to check out some books and does not bring her cell phone.
- Mom goes to pick up milk at the grocery store and does not tell me how long it will take.
- Mom takes the dog on a walk for 10 minutes, with her cell phone.
- Mom goes to the mailbox at the end of the block to mail a letter.

> **EASY BUTTON:** Have your parents start with a very brief errand, such as walking to the mailbox at the end of the block to mail a letter. You can even have them run an "errand" in the garage or neighbor's yard.

 ## DARE 23 — PLACE AN ORDER BY YOURSELF

Today, being brave is about to get a little more delicious: Place an order at a restaurant all by yourself. To get the most out of this Dare, be sure to:

- Stand in line alone
- Order with a cashier instead of ordering online
- Speak in a clear, loud voice
- Pick up your order and pay yourself

If you're not sure how to order or pay for food, ask your parents for instructions before you hop in line, or watch the people ordering ahead of you.

 **DOUBLE DARE:** Order a "secret menu item." That Pink Drink from a certain coffee chain, anyone?

 ## DARE 24 — ATTEND A SLEEPOVER

There is nothing better than hanging out with awesome people in pajamas. And you can make the PJ party last all night by going to a sleepover with a friend or family member!

YOUR PAJAMA PARTY CHECKLIST:
- ☐ PAJAMAS, OBVIOUSLY
- ☐ POPCORN
- ☐ GAMES
- ☐ COZY SOCKS
- ☐ FAVE PILLOW
- ☐ SOMEONE ELSE'S HOUSE

EASY BUTTON: If a sleepover feels too hard to start, try a "sleepunder" or "lateover" where you stay into the evening with no possibility of pickup until a certain time.

Chapter 4 • Doing Stuff Alone (Separation Anxiety) • 55

WALK OR BIKE SOMEPLACE BY YOURSELF

These Crocs are made for walking, and that's just what they'll do! Take yourself on a wander around your neighborhood all by your lonesome self.

Work with your parent to plan out a path and think about how far other kids your age can go on their own. If walking is not your thing, grab a set of wheels and turn that solo walk into a bike ride!

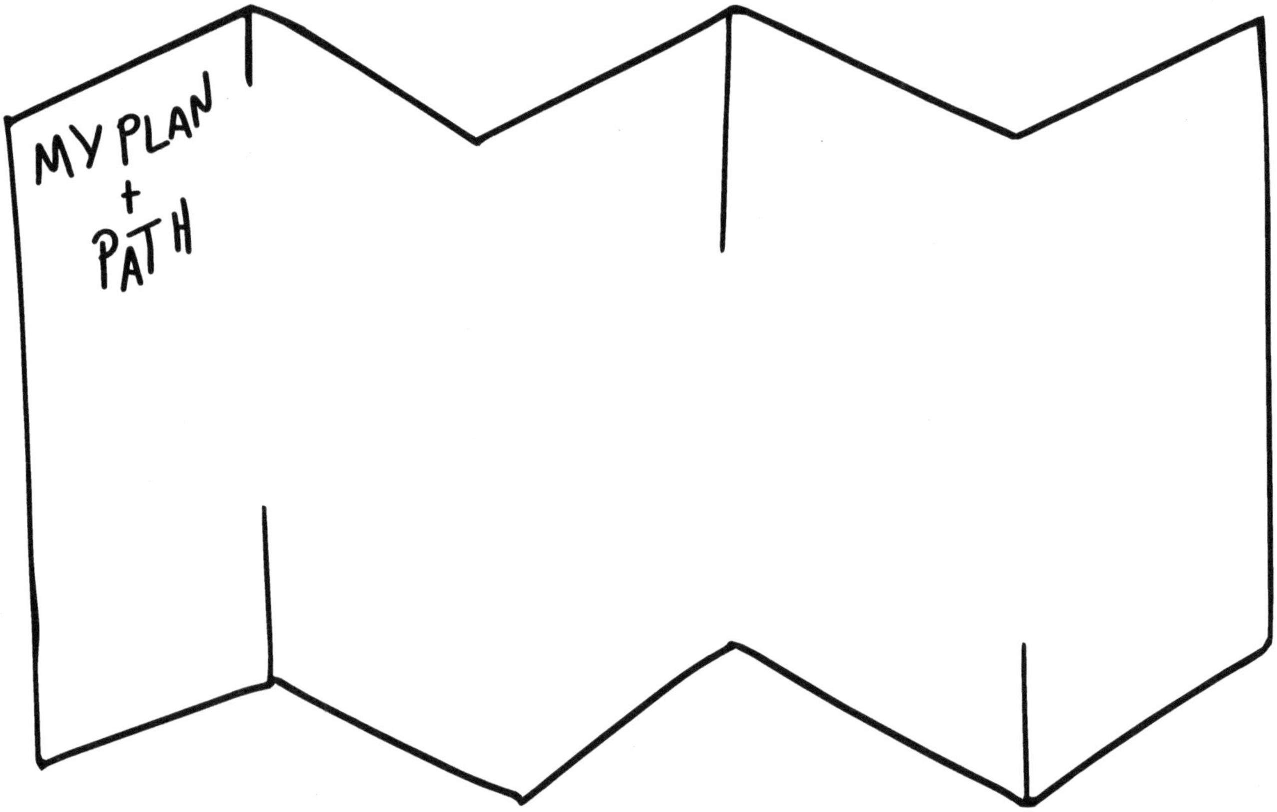

MY PLAN + PATH

DARE 26: PLAY BIRTHDAY PARTY BINGO

Wrap a present, put on your best party outfit, and head out to celebrate someone's special day! While you're there, play Birthday Party Bingo and see how many of the separation challenges on the bingo sheet below you can complete before the party is over. You can mark this Dare as complete if you get all the Dares in a single row done, but extra credit goes to those who can get the entire sheet finished!

Attend the party for the full length.	Pick out a snack without your parent.	Play in a different room or area for 10 minutes.	Play with another party guest for 20 minutes.	Talk to an unfamiliar adult without your parent next to you.
Get a plate of food alone.	Go to the bathroom alone.	Ask the name of someone you don't know without your parent nearby.	Say "Happy birthday" to the guest of honor without a parent by you.	Participate in a birthday activity without your parent nearby.
Talk to an unfamiliar adult while your parent is next to you.	Play outside for 10 minutes while your parent is still inside.	Free space!	Play in a different room/area for 5 minutes.	Sit at a different table than your parent while eating cake.
Find where the gifts go and put your gift down by yourself.	Play with guests for 15 minutes while your parent wanders the party.	Participate in a birthday activity with your parent nearby.	Thank the host of the party without your parent nearby.	Have your parent go to the bathroom alone.
"Lose" your parent on purpose at the party for 15 minutes.	Ask your parent to step out of the party for 10 minutes.	Go alone to get your parent a snack.	Sing "Happy Birthday" without your parent next to you.	Offer to help clean up food plates without your parent.

 **CARPOOL**

Take a step toward saving the planet today by trying out that magical eco-friendly thing called carpooling! Get dropped off somewhere by someone other than your parents. Maximize the fun on this Dare by picking a friend or another extra special family member to do the driving. Bonus points if you get to use a carpool lane on the freeway.

Try a car-friendly game while you're at it:

ALPHABET RACES: Race against your seat mates to spot every letter of the alphabet on your drive. When you see the letter, call it out along with where you see it ("A: Apple on the billboard"). First person to Z wins!

TWENTY QUESTIONS: Crown one person the Answerer and ask them to think of a person, place, or thing. All other players in the car are the Questioners. The Questioners can ask up to 20 yes-or-no questions to figure out what the Answerer is thinking of. Get creative with those questions to make sure you don't use all 20!

TWO TRUTHS AND A LIE: Try this game with car-mates that you don't know well (yet!). Each person takes turns sharing two truths and one lie about themselves. Your car buddies try to guess which statement is the lie.

DARE 28) GO INTO ORBIT AT THE GROCERY STORE

If your mom's shopping cart is mission control, you be the spaceship: Go into orbit at the grocery store.

Try scouting out the next aisle down and report back with any foods you've found that you might need to get. Even better, go on short missions for your parent, finding items they have on the grocery list.

Chapter 4 • Doing Stuff Alone (Separation Anxiety) • 59

 ## GO RADIO SILENT

Pretend it's the olden days, that ancient time they called BC: Before Cellphones. That's right, ditch the cell phone and pick a two-hour time frame where your parents will not respond to your calls or texts.

Have your parent run an errand while you hang with a friend or do something else fun. While you're apart, tell your parents not to check their phones, or better yet, ask them to leave their phones at home.

Will Worry tell you that there is going to be some "unhandleable" emergency where you'll need to talk to your parents RIGHT AWAY? Of course.

What if you throw up? What if you find a lost dog and don't know who the owner is? What if something bad happens? What if those two hours are the exact two hours that aliens decide to attack?!

Is an emergency possible? Sure. But remember, plenty of grown-ups in your life survived their *entire childhood* without cell phones, and they figured out how to handle any tricky situations that came up. You can too!

 Your parents can respond to one check-in text during that two-hour window.

 ## DARE 30: TAKE AN IN-HOUSE CAMPING TRIP

Roll out the sleeping bag, grab a flashlight, pack your backpack with books and snacks, and eat a few marshmallows (but probably don't start a fire)—it's time for an in-house camping trip.

Try sleeping in a different location in your house, farther away from your parents than usual. If you're a kid who usually sleeps with Mom and Dad in bed, this might look like sleeping right next to the bed instead. If you sleep in your own room, this might involve decking out the basement for a sleepover of one. Either way, try to fall asleep all on your own in this new space after you go through your goodnight routine.

NOTE: Blanket fort tents strongly encouraged.

SEPARATION BRAVERY BADGE

Check all those boxes?

CONGRATULATIONS! You have earned your Separation Bravery Badge.

EXTRA CREDIT

Still want more? Try out a few Extra Credit Dares below:

⇨ Play hide-and-seek in a public place, like a store, park, or mall.

⇨ Go to sports practice or a game without a parent in attendance.

⇨ Use a public restroom alone, with your parent standing nearby or outside.

⇨ Ask a new person or extended family member to pick you up after school.

CHAPTER 5
(im)Perfection and Mistakez
(Perfectionism)

Have you ever had the feeling that you *must* get that perfect score on your test, or score every shot you take, or make a grand total of . . . wait for it . . . zero mistakes while performing in the band concert? If so, you've sampled one of the extra tricky flavors of Worry: perfectionism.

What Is Perfectionism?

Perfectionism is the belief that you need to do everything exactly right, all the time. Kids who wrestle with perfectionism hold themselves to the highest standards, above and beyond the expectations of teachers, coaches, and parents. With perfectionism on board, even regular days become ultra-stressful, because a perfectionist feels like they are living on the edge. They feel deep in their bones that if they have even a hair out of place, their world will come crashing down around them and life as they know it will be forever changed.

Worry's Tricks for Perfectionism

For this chapter, I would like to introduce you to Worry's fussy cousin: Dr. Perfect. When it comes to perfectionism, it's Dr. Perfect who tells you that you can't possibly handle the judgment, criticism, or "bad job feelings" that can come with mistakes or failure.

BRAVER KID

Dr. Perfect: If you make a mistake, it will haunt you for the rest of your life and you will NEVER recover!

Braver Kid: Geez, this guy is a bit dramatic.

Dr. Perfect: If you don't look perfectly put together, with your room set up just right, and if you don't do the right thing, EVERYONE WILL JUDGE YOU AND NEVER TALK TO YOU AGAIN!

Braver Kid: Okay . . . fine . . . really dramatic . . .

Dr. Perfect: Worst of all . . . I don't even want to say it, but if you maybe possibly ever fail (*gasp*), then EVERYTHING IS RUINED FOR EVER AND EVER AND EVER AND EVER AND . . .

Braver Kid: Yikes. Just yikes.

WHAT ARE SOME THINGS THAT DR. PERFECT SAYS TO YOU ABOUT MISTAKES?

Hello, this is Dr. Perfect calling. Guess what . . .

64 • The Be Brave Activity Book

Dr. Perfect's Demand

Once Dr. Perfect has convinced you that you can't handle mistakes or failure, he follows up with an "easy" solution:

Don't ever. Ever. EVER. Make any mistakes.

Dr. Perfect can feel extra hard to argue with because teachers and parents are always telling kids to try hard, and everyone wants to do well!

Making sure you perform perfectly can seem like a good idea. After all, who wouldn't want to get 100 percent on the test? To make every shot they take in a basketball game? To never have a spot of food on their shirt or a hair out of place? When we perform perfectly, it feels a lot like winning—and parents, teachers, or other kids usually congratulate us on our success when we do so well.

However, it's not that simple.

Why Perfectionism Is a Trap

The trouble is, Dr. Perfect forgets to mention that if you want to get really good at something or learn something new, you usually have to fail many times before you succeed.

Here are some examples of things that EVERYONE has failed at a lot before they succeeded:

- First words
- First steps
- First time trying to read
- First time hula hooping
- First time riding a bike
- First time doing a new dance
- First time playing the piano
- First time skiing

Dr. Perfect wants to be 100 percent sure that you never make mistakes so that no one ever judges you to be anything less than perfect. However, if you try to make *absolutely sure* that you never ever *ever* make a mistake—that no one *ever* critiques you or judges you or that you *never* feel the sting of your own disappointment from a less-than-perfect performance—then you will be stuck only doing things you already know how to do well.

That means . . .

No setting any hard-but-exciting goals that have even the slightest chance of not working out. Professional basketball player? YouTuber? Astronaut? Nope. Failure is just too likely.

No taking any classes that are interesting but hard. Learning hard stuff is just too risky. What if you get a B?!

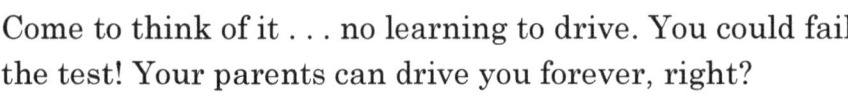

No learning to ride a bike. You've got walking perfected, so no wheels for you.

Come to think of it . . . no learning to drive. You could fail the test! Your parents can drive you forever, right?

No trying rock climbing.

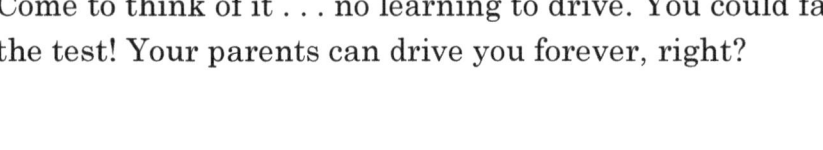

Or a new-to-you video game!

Or bowling!

Or that one funny game with the trampoline and the ball.

You could mess up the rules or look weird! It does look fun, though.

Avoiding mistakes and staying in control feels like the safe thing to do, but it's actually the riskiest thing of all because it stops you from doing the things that can take you to MAXIMUM FUN AND AWESOMENESS. How, you ask?

Imagine you have a one-gallon jug, the kind that might hold milk. Got it? Now imagine it is instead filled to the top with glitter—go ahead and pick only your favorite colors for your glitter mix. Each one of those pieces of glitter is a minute of your time, and the whole jug is all of the time you get in a single day.

Now imagine you have a bunch of buckets in front of you. Each bucket is something important to you: There's a family bucket, a friends bucket, a school bucket, and a fun bucket. You might have extra buckets for other things that matter to you, like learning to play piano, or video games, or sports, or playing with your dog.

DRAW YOUR BUCKETS HERE.

You can pour your time into those buckets however you want—it's your time, after all! If you choose, you could spend all 24 hours of your day playing with your dog Fluffy. But you only get one jug of time each day . . . and that's where Dr. Perfect gets in the way.

OBVIOUSLY THE RIGHT CALL.

Chapter 5 • (im)Perfection and Mistakez (Perfectionism) • 67

He says if you *juuust* pour all of your glitter into the buckets he cares about—like the piano-playing bucket or the spelling test bucket—then he *promises* that you'll never make any mistakes, which will keep you safe from those horrible feelings of disappointment or failure. Perfect spelling test, here you come! All you need to do is devote every ounce of your time to that bucket for the next 10 hours.

This will, of course, give you a great shot at a successful spelling test. However, if you do this, you'll have no glitter left to pour into any other buckets. Listening to Dr. Perfect about spelling leaves no time for that math assignment due tomorrow, no time for family movie night with buttery popcorn, no time for soccer practice, and no time for petting Fluffy. Dr. Perfect sucks away your time from what matters.

What's more is that his promises are lies. No one can live a perfect life totally free from mistakes. In fact, mistakes are a *normal* part of learning, growing, and trying new things!

Guess Who

Here are a few examples of people who struggled, made mistakes, and failed at things that mattered to them. Can you guess who they are?

I didn't learn to speak until I was 2. At 8, a teacher told me I would "never succeed." When I was 16, I made enough mistakes that I failed the entrance exam for the college I applied to. I graduated near the bottom of my class. I was the only one in my class with no job offer after graduation. I failed the military's entrance exam. I almost dropped out of college at 21. I believe that "I have no talents, I am only passionately curious."

 More than 12 publishers rejected my first book before one agreed to publish it. Even then, the publisher told me to "get a day job" because I could never make a living writing children's books.

 Oh yeah? My first book was rejected 30 TIMES!

 Looking at my list, I might be the least successful politician ever:
- 1832: Defeated for state election
- 1838: Defeated to be the House speaker
- 1843: Defeated for nomination for Congress
- 1846: Lost re-election to Congress
- 1856: Defeated for US Senate
- 1858: Defeated for nomination for vice president
- 1858: Defeated for US Senate

 I was fired from my job as a reporter for a Baltimore news program. They told me I was "unfit for television news."

I was fired from the Kansas City Star newspaper in 1919. My editor told me I "lacked imagination and had no good ideas." I started an animation studio that ended up bankrupt.

 At 14, I was turned down for casting call after casting call. People said my nose was too big and my eyes were too small. I remember some people telling me that I could never be on a magazine cover. It made me feel insecure.

 I auditioned for a band while I worked as a truck driver. I must not have performed well because I didn't get in. They told me, "Stick to driving trucks in Memphis because you're never going to make it as a singer."

 I made enough mistakes that I was cut from my high school basketball team. My coach said I had "a lack of skill."

Answers: Albert Einstein, J. K. Rowling, Stephen King, Abraham Lincoln, Oprah Winfrey, Walt Disney, Giselle Bundchen, Elvis Presley, Michael Jordan

Chapter 5 • (im)Perfection and Mistakez (Perfectionism) • 69

What Dr. Perfect Actually Can Guarantee

While Dr. Perfect can never guarantee that you won't make a mistake, there are a few things you can be sure of if you listen to Dr. Perfect:

#1) YOU'LL PROCRASTINATE: If you're not 100 percent sure that you won't make a mistake on something, or the risk of failure feels really scary, you might decide to avoid working on the activity at all. Hello, procrastination! When you procrastinate, it guarantees that you'll feel more stressed out as the due date, recital, or deadline gets closer. If you avoid studying for that exam, practicing for your piano recital, or working on that school project, you actually can be SURE that you will never get better!

#2) YOU'LL GIVE UP: Dr. Perfect will sometimes tell you that if you can't get something exactly right then you shouldn't even bother trying. For example, if you dream of playing basketball but let Dr. Perfect convince you it's too risky to try out, you can be SURE you will never play on the team!

Wait, those guarantees sound terrible . . .

What to Do Instead

Instead of listening to Dr. Perfect and letting him decide where all that glitter goes each day, you need to show him who's boss by taking back control of your time. That means . . .

PRACTICE GETTING TO "GOOD ENOUGH."

Good enough means that you pour just enough glitter into your bucket to move toward your goal so you can save the rest for other things that matter to you. That means you might:

- Study for the test for two hours instead of four, just like the teacher said to!
- Follow the instructor's directions for a 30-minute bongo practice, even if your performance is not yet mistake-free at the end of your practice!
- Cross out the spelling mistake on your homework assignment and continue to work on it, instead of tearing up the paper and starting over!

At first, good enough might feel uncomfortable. Dr. Perfect will certainly try to throw a tantrum about it. But if you practice stopping at good enough, you might start to see that Dr. Perfect's predictions aren't coming true and that good enough usually gets you where you want to go, giving you more time for fun.

And, since Dr. Perfect's most common trick is to tell you that you cannot possibly handle making a mistake, the best thing you can do to shrink him and take charge is . . .

If you practice making and handling mistakes and the feelings that come with them, you mistake-proof yourself. A mistake-proofed kid can let any "whoops" moments roll off their back. They get up and keep moving toward what matters to them even when they don't succeed at first.

Best of all, mistake-proofed kids get to live their life to the fullest, whether it's taking that fun-but-challenging pottery class, playing on the advanced soccer team, or running for student president—and maybe even winning!

The most powerful thing you can do to quiet Dr. Perfect is to make mistakes *on purpose*, which makes them feel less scary over time. And just like other types of anxiety, the best way to do this is through practice! Are you ready to get perfectly imperfect, make some mistakes, and go for good enough?

Operation Oopsies, here we come!

 **LET FAILURE HAPPEN**

Faculty at Stanford and Harvard created the term *failure deprived* to describe a phenomenon they have observed growing in youth in recent years: students who are exceptional in their academic and extracurricular record but who seem unable to cope with any degree of failure or struggle. Failure-deprived kids experience success at every turn, but they are fragile and anxious because they have no sense of their ability to handle life's setbacks. Like a rubber band never asked to stretch, these kids can become rigid and brittle, breaking at the first pressure point they experience.

Kids *need* to experience mistakes, to lose, and to receive negative feedback early on in order to learn that they can cope with failure and the feelings that go with it! As a parent, your job is not to prevent your child's failure by acting as an on-call personal tutor, coach, or instructor. Instead, your job is to act as a support and a resource for your kid while they struggle—being there to talk to them about the difficulty without controlling the outcome. Let your child struggle during the exercises that follow, and instead of trying to talk them into feeling better, give them your own vote of confidence: "I know this feels hard, and I believe you can handle it, whatever the outcome."

Perfectionism: Dares

DARE 31 — PAINT AN IMPERFECT SELF-PORTRAIT

Gather up your brushes, grab an easel, make like Picasso, and paint an IMPERFECT self-portrait. Paint with your opposite hand: If you're a righty, use your left hand. If you're a lefty, use your right hand.

As you paint, maybe you put your ears where your nose is. Maybe you make your face blue and green and just a little too pointy. Maybe you use too much paint, too little paint, or no paint at all! Maybe you paint with different colors of frosting while using your tongue as a brush (yum?). The world is your (imperfect) canvas! Go forth and art yourself.

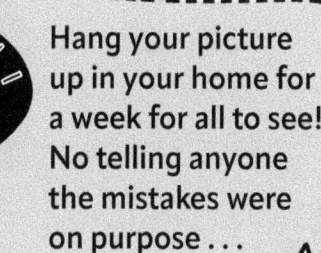

> Hang your picture up in your home for a week for all to see! No telling anyone the mistakes were on purpose . . .

DARE 32 — START A "NO" COLLECTION

Has Worry ever tried to stop you from asking about what you want because . . . "What if they say no?" This Dare asks you to get "nos" on purpose! Let's see if getting rejected is really as bad as Worry says it is. Here are a few ideas to get you started:

- Ask a parent if you can have ice cream for dinner.
- Ask a teacher if you can build a blanket fort in the classroom.
- Ask an employee if you can make an announcement on the store intercom.
- Ask a neighbor if you can borrow their dog for the week.

Collecting nos is basically a rejection scavenger hunt. How many can you collect in one hour? In one day? At the mall? At school?

Total no count: _____

Favorite question asked: _____

Favorite no response: _____

What most surprised you: _____

 **GET A QUESTION WRONG**

Instead of making sure that you answer every question correctly, try out the feeling of "wrong answer." Worry might tell you that anything less than perfect is a failure, or that your teacher will judge you for that mistake, but here's the truth:

- Mistakes are proof that you are growing and learning new things.
- Mistakes are normal, especially when you start taking classes that challenge you and make you smarter.
- Mistakes are helpful—they are one of the best opportunities to learn!

Today, practice sitting with the feeling that shows up when you make a mistake by getting a question wrong on your homework on purpose!

Does this feel tricky? Work up to a "wrong answer" with the sample ladder below:

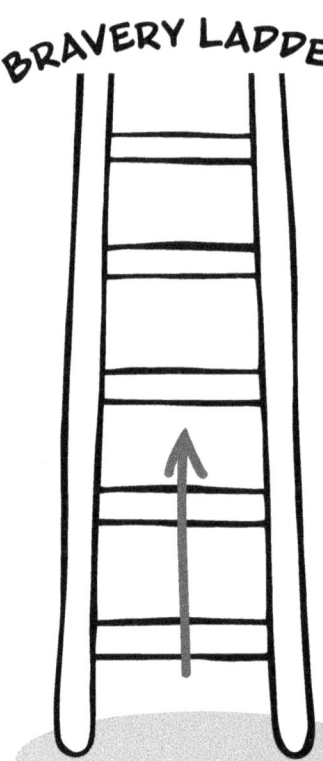

- Get a quiz or test question wrong in a class where it might impact your grade.
- Get a question wrong in a class where you think the teacher will notice.
- Get a test question wrong where your class grade won't change.
- Get a homework question wrong where your class grade won't change.
- Write in the wrong answer on an ungraded assignment.
- Answer a question with a "might-be-right" answer—no double-checking or figuring out if you've nailed it.
- Misspell words and use messy handwriting when putting down the right answer to a homework question.

 Pick a class where your grade won't be affected.

DARE 34: MESS UP THIS PAGE

No perfect workbooks allowed—let's see if you can RUIN this page! Do your worst, and in case you need some ideas:

- Poke holes in the page to let some light in. Words need sunlight to grow!
- Smear some food on a bit of the page. Can you get a fingerprint to show up in that barbecue sauce stain? *Wait, no . . . that's plants. But maybe poke some holes anyway?*
- Pretend this page has instructions for a secret mission. Use a dark-colored marker to "redact" words so no one knows what you were told!
- Coffee cup stains are nice circular stain options . . .
- Crumple the page! It will never lay flat again! Muahahahaha!
- Rip off a piece of the page and glue it back on in a different spot.
- Doodle all over the place—in *pen*!
- Tear off a strip of the page and make a bravery bracelet for yourself, you daring, paper-tearing champion.

Now step back and admire your imperfect work. This book will never be the same!

Chapter 5 • (im)Perfection and Mistakez (Perfectionism) • 75

> Hi there! This page was left blank on purpose, so that when you mess up the page before it you don't lose any information for the next dare.

> Yes! You can really go for it! Ruin away!

BE A NEWBIE

Get outside your comfort zone and try an activity you have never done before! When you're learning something new, mistakes are unavoidable (but maybe just a little fun too?). Consider all the things you could try for the first time:

- Learn to juggle.
- Speak a new language.
- Go rock climbing.
- Learn a new dance.
- Cook a new food.
- Learn to whistle.
- Throw a football spiral.
- Play Dungeons and Dragons.
- Try a new sport.
- Attend chess club at school.
- Play the trombone.
- Try a new board game with friends.

 **When you make a mistake in your new activity, smile and point it out to someone! "Whoops, I really goofed that up!"**

Chapter 5 • (im)Perfection and Mistakez (Perfectionism) • 77

DARE 36
MESS UP SOMEONE'S NAME

> ROSES ARE RED
>
> VIOLETS ARE BLUE
>
> MESS UP THE NAME
>
> OF THAT KID TALKING TO YOU!

How many times has Worry stopped you from talking to someone because you weren't 100 percent sure of that person's name? For this Dare, make a name blunder on purpose. I know it sounds awkward, but you've totally got this, Bob. I mean Bill. Wait. Have we met before?

CORRECT NAME → **WRONG NAME**

"What are you doing in our house, Goldenlakes?"

"Gandilucks? Guiltyleaks?"

"...Girl?"

78 • The Be Brave Activity Book

DARE 37: MAKE A "GOOD ENOUGH" THANK YOU CARD

Be just the right amount of courteous today and create a "good enough" thank you card for someone. Maybe you could thank Aunt Katie for the 400 pairs of socks she sent you for your birthday, or thank your friend for always providing the most impressive and forceful high fives on Earth (ouch . . .).

Whoever you pick, your job is to make the thank you card good enough. A "good enough" thank you card means:

- You make a card that is nice, not THE MOST PERFECT THANK YOU CARD OF ALL TIME.
- You spend 5 minutes, not 45 minutes, thinking of what to say.
- You write the card out ONCE, not until the handwriting is exactly right.
- No rulers allowed—let the lines be wobbly!
- You let any imperfections stick around instead of starting over. Cross out that misspelled word and keep going! In pen!

DOUBLE DARE: Write the card with messy handwriting, or add an Oopsies and misspell the person's name (or your own) on the envelope.

Chapter 5 • (im)Perfection and Mistakez (Perfectionism) • 79

 ## DARE 38: CREATE A MISTAKES JAR

By now, you've heard the phrase "practice makes perfect," but what you probably don't know is that the best kind of practice is actually *never* perfect because the most important part of practice *is* mistakes. This Dare challenges you to celebrate those mistakes as a sign of progress!

#1 Get two jars and fill one up with beads of different colors and sizes. This is your "mistakes to make" jar. The empty jar is the "mistakes I have made."

#2 The next time you practice a skill you want to get better at, like shooting free throws, playing an instrument, or reading hard words, move a bead into the "mistakes I have made" jar every time an oopsies occurs. If it's an extra big mistake, you can pick an extra special bead to move.

#3 When your "mistakes I have made" jar is full, reward yourself for accomplishing all those wonderful mistakes and see how much better at your skill you have become!

Full Jar Reward: _____

DID YOU KNOW?

For most skills, the only way to get really, really good at them is by making enough mistakes to move all the beads into the second jar. The fastest way to do this is to focus on practicing the parts of the skill that are hard for you!

 Before starting this challenge, record yourself trying out your skill to show how good (or not so good!) you are at the beginning. Then record yourself again after filling your mistakes jar and check your progress!

DARE 39. LIVE IN CHAOS

It's a wild and crazy world out there, and today you're going to make sure of it! Embrace the chaos around you and prove to yourself that chaos can't stop you from living your life. For one day, try these on for size:

- Hang up a picture or poster crooked in your house.
- Mess up a display in your room. (Those completed LEGO sets are begging for a change!)
- Pull your curtains or blinds so they are not even.
- Unmake your bed. (Yes, parents, you heard right!)
- While you are at it, *un*tidy your room!
- Mix up the food on your plate so it's scrambled together.
- Wear an imperfect outfit for the day. I'm talking about a shirt inside out, a little food stain on your pants, or a bunch of patterns that feel zany to you. Get wild!

Chapter 5 • (im)Perfection and Mistakez (Perfectionism)

# DARE 40 — TAKE AN IMPERFECT PORTRAIT

Skip the filters or photo editing today and share a beautifully untouched picture of yourself with friends and family. Ready?

Have a parent take a photo of you RIGHT THIS VERY SECOND! Now! No fixing your hair, tweaking the lighting, or changing your outfit. Then text or email that photo to 10 friends and family members with a friendly caption (like "Happy Wednesday!").

Some common questions you might have at this point:

Q: Umm, okay, but does it have to be right now?

A: Yes! Don't let Worry stop you. Embrace the you-ness of you right now, imperfections and all! But, uh, if your parent is driving a car, maybe have them pull over first.

Q: Can I take the photo with my parents too?

A: Sure. But they can't fix their hair or change the lighting either.

Q: Can my cat or dog or bird or pet alligator also be in the photo?

A: Yes, obviously! Photos involving pets are strongly encouraged. But don't let your alligator fix their hair.

Q: Instead of texting the photo to 10 people, can I have my parents post it to a social media account?

A: Totally. Remember, though, the goal of this challenge is to practice getting comfortable with imperfection. If you post this photo to a site like Instagram that has lots of filters, your goal is to post the photo *as is*, not through a beautiful-but-fake filter.

 Pick friends and family who have already seen you at your most and least polished!

82 • The Be Brave Activity Book

IMPERFECTION BRAVERY BADGE

Check all those boxes?

CONGRATULATIONS! You have earned your
Imperfection Bravery Badge.

EXTRA CREDIT

Still want more? Try out a few Extra Credit Dares below:

➪ Scribble out a word when writing an assignment in pen.

➪ Work at an unorganized desk.

➪ Wear your hair in a messy style.

➪ Send a text with a misspelled word.

➪ Lace up one of your shoes incorrectly.

CHAPTER 6
Spooky Stuff (Phobias)

Everybody has things that scare them at different ages and stages. If you are 3 years old, getting on a plane to fly to Grandma and Grandpa's house is likely no big deal (ooh, a nice grown-up with a snack cart!), and you probably have all the confidence of Beyoncé when belting out your personal version of "Wheels on the Bus" . . . in front of all the people in the department store . . . at FULL volume. However, Mommy going to the store, or Daddy leaving you alone at night? Or, heaven forbid, going *poop* on the potty?! Terrifying. However, if you are 13 years old, the exact opposite may be true: Mom and Dad running an errand, sleeping in your own room, and doing your business in the bathroom is NBD, but flying 30,000 feet in the air in a metal object that's going 600 miles an hour, with no ability to steer the plane? That might be pretty spooky. And the prospect of singing? Out loud? In front of other random people? Um, no. Just no.

These changing fears are normal and a part of growing up, like a brief storm on a warm summer day. However, sometimes those regular-kid scaries like thunderstorms, insects, or heights get supersized, growing so big that they start to take over your thoughts throughout the day, week, or month. These mega worries are called *phobias*.

What Is a Phobia?

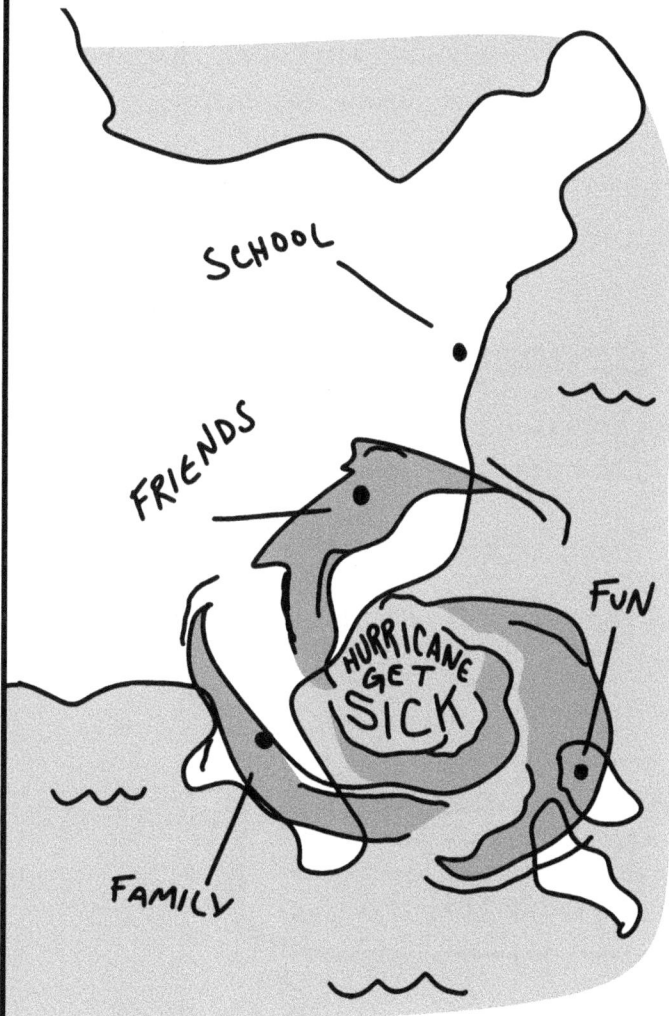

A phobia is a jumbo fear, the hurricane of Worry Storms. The fear is focused on one specific thing, but because the fear is so strong, the arms of that Worry Storm reach out and start to disrupt other parts of your life.

For example, a lot of kids are anxious about throwing up. No one likes it, it's uncomfortable, and throwing up in public or at school gets a lot of attention. (Note: If you are looking for a way to create a distraction and some adult chaos, hug your stomach while saying to the nearest adult, "I think I'm gonna *puuuke!*") But a person with a phobia of vomiting is not only *worried* about throwing up, they are *terrified* of it. Their anxious thoughts about vomiting don't just show up when they are sick, but every single day. In fact, Worry gets so loud about throwing up that they start to avoid doing things that matter to them, like playing sports or going to sleepovers. Sometimes, Worry gets so feisty about the possibility of throwing up that it feels risky to do even everyday things, like participating in gym class, eating a full meal in the lunchroom, or watching a movie.

With phobias, whenever you come face to face with your feared situation or thing, it causes your body's alarm system to turn on full blast, right away, even when there is no immediate danger—hello, instant False Alarm Feelings! (See chapter 1 for more on the physical feelings that show up with anxiety.)

Someone might throw up in the film and then YOU might throw up! Don't watch it!

Even more annoying, just *thinking* about these jumbo fears can actually turn on your body's alarm system all by itself. That's because when your brain thinks about a phobia, it feels like the scary thing is about to occur *right now*.

Chapter 6 • Spooky Stuff (Phobias) • 85

It feels like you're mere moments away from being stung by a bee, falling from a height, or being struck by lightning. As a result, your fight-or-flight response turns on, which means that your heart starts to beat faster and faster, you get all sweaty and shaky, you start to feel hot, and you may even get nauseous as your brain presses pause on digestion (extra frustrating if you happen to be afraid of, well, nausea!). These physical feelings only ramp your anxiety up more and can even turn into a full-on panic attack. (For more on panic, see chapter 9.)

Worry's Tricks for Spooky Stuff

The main trick that Worry will use with most phobias is to convince you that there is danger ahead—in BIG FLASHING CAPITAL letters.

Worry may trick you into thinking that:

 Something TERRIBLE will happen if you come in contact with the spooky thing, even if the terrible thing is very unlikely.

> If you get too close, that dog will definitely BITE YOU! It will chomp down so hard, and that will hurt so much, and then you'll have to go to the hospital and get stitches, and you might never again have all your fingers, and your friends will start calling you Ol' 9 Fingers and . . .

 The spooky thing is a HUGE DEAL, when it is really a little deal.

> If you go to the doctor, you will have to get a SHOT, and it will be THE MOST PAINFUL THING EVER! Nothing can be worse than this!

#3 You'll be so afraid of the spooky thing that you won't be able to handle the scary and uncomfortable feelings . . . when actually, you can.

> Seeing a snake in real life would be just TOO MUCH! It will hiss and move, and then you'll feel so scared that the scared feeling will NEVER STOP! YOU ABSOLUTELY CANNOT HANDLE THIS!

Worry posts up signs all around that say "Turn back now!" or "Doom lies that way!" and plasters everything with caution tape. But, of course, Worry has its magnifying glass out, making small risks seem like big spiky pits of danger and doom. Consider the common fears below. What prediction does your Worry make about each of these?

Spiders	Snakes	Flying

Heights	Throwing up	Bugs

Needles	The doctor or dentist

Chapter 6 • Spooky Stuff (Phobias) • 87

Worry's Spooky Demands

Worry acts like a misguided crossing guard, telling you about all the danger that lies ahead and trying to talk you into terror. Then, Worry tries to shepherd you to safety . . . which, of course means avoidance. It makes demands like:

WHAT SPOOKY STUFF DOES WORRY TELL YOU TO AVOID?

Why Avoidance Keeps Spooky Stuff Spooky

The problem with avoidance is that while it provides relief by making you feel safe in the short term, it never allows you to find out what REALLY lies beyond the caution tape that Worry posted. You never get to see for yourself how truly dangerous the spooky thing actually is.

FACT CHECK: If you tune in to that smart and clever part of your brain and look around, are other people your age able to handle the spooky thing? Do you see other kids trying out the rock wall at the climbing gym, getting their vaccine, or petting that big shaggy dog? If other kids are trying it and handling it, it's a good sign that Worry is exaggerating the risk, making things feel more dangerous than they really are.

What to Do Instead

Instead of using Worry's "Turn back now!" signs as your only source of information, check in with your smart brain and other people you trust.

If the following are true . . .

- ☐ Other kids are trying it out.
- ☐ Your parents are confident that the situation is safe.
- ☐ Your teacher or coach is allowing it.
- ☐ You know that Worry might be tricking you.

. . . then you have permission to ignore those Worry signposts and forge ahead! Take small and manageable steps in the direction of the spooky thing, and prove to yourself how handleable it actually is.

NEXT UP:
Dares to get you started.

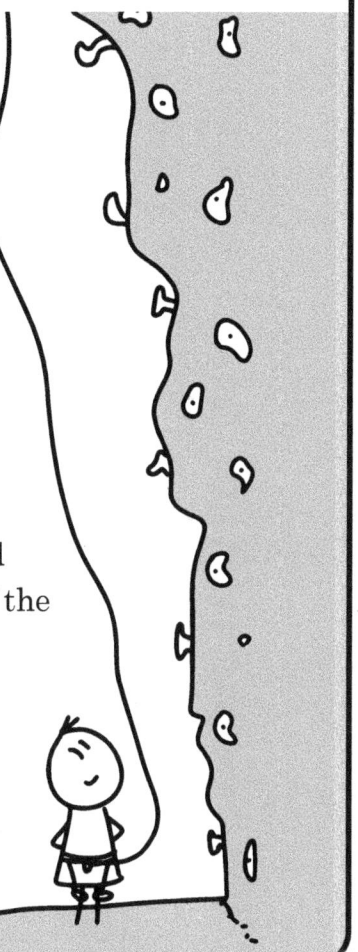

 LOOK OUT FOR SAFETY BEHAVIORS

If your kid is working up the courage to face a fear that is age-typical but outsized, be on the lookout for safety behaviors. A safety behavior is something that a person does in an attempt to keep themselves safe from the scary outcome that Worry is predicting. For example, if Worry is predicting that your child is going to throw up in a class (catastrophe!), they might:

- Avoid "high-risk" situations like hard running in gym class
- Avoid eating in the lunchroom
- Avoid eating a full meal
- Avoid touching doorknobs that are "germy"
- Start tuning in to stomach sensations more frequently
- Start taking more frequent trips to the bathroom
- Start carrying anti-nausea chews or bracelets
- Start becoming a "frequent flier" in the nurse's office

Or if Worry is predicting that your child will be stung by a bee (too painful! could never handle!), they might:

- Avoid playing in yards with gardens
- Avoid walking near garbage cans in parks
- Avoid eating fruits and sweet foods outside
- Avoid wearing bright "flower" colors
- Start requesting to play inside more
- Start insisting on long sleeves and pants outdoors
- Start asking adults about whether there are bees or gardens nearby
- Start maintaining a "minimum distance" when bees are present

Safety behaviors are a form of avoidance that interferes with the learning that takes place during bravery-building exposures (a.k.a. Dares). Think of safety-behavior-filled learning as swiss-cheese learning: Kids are gaining *some* confidence in their capacity, but there are a lot of holes in that confidence.

With a safety behavior, your child's brain does not register that "It's very unlikely I will throw up at school. This is safe." Instead, a safety-behavior-filled exposure teaches their brain that "Okay, I probably won't throw up at school, but *only if* I don't eat meals at school, never participate in gym class, and eat my anti-nausea chews all day. These actions are keeping me safe."

The longer kids use safety behaviors, the more strongly they will believe that the safety behaviors are what they *have* to do in order to stay safe. Safety behaviors are also a bit addictive—the more you use one, the more safety behaviors you will feel like you need. You might start out by checking that your screen door is closed to keep out those bees, but eventually it will become the front *and* back door, then all the windows, and then you'll take on a second job as the family door monitor, ensuring that everyone closes the door quickly behind them (QUICKLY!) . . .

When practicing any brave challenge, encourage your kid to "fade out" their safety behaviors—to drop them one at a time, easiest first. Quit the job as door monitor and take it down to "just" a double check of the doors, then try opening the windows to let in the breeze, and eventually leave the screen door open for a bit. Each step forward will build up their confidence and allow all that bravery building to occur in the brain, free from the swiss-cheese learning that safety behaviors create.

Spooky Stuff: Dares

DARE 41 — GO ON A SPIDER SAFARI

Have you ever heard of a safari? Going on a safari means going on an expedition into the wilderness, camera in hand, to look for and observe interesting wildlife.

Most people think about safaris as an adventure where you drive through African grasslands, but today you are going to adventure closer to home, trying to capture on film the most classic of all spooky things: spiders.

Grab a camera and a flashlight, wander into your backyard or basement, and go on a spider safari. Scope alongside those nooks, crannies, corners, and weeds where you think you are most likely to find these eight-legged friends hiding. See if you can find three different spiders doing interesting things, and get photos for proof!

Places to check:
- The weeds
- Near the fence
- Corners of the garage
- Basement windowsills

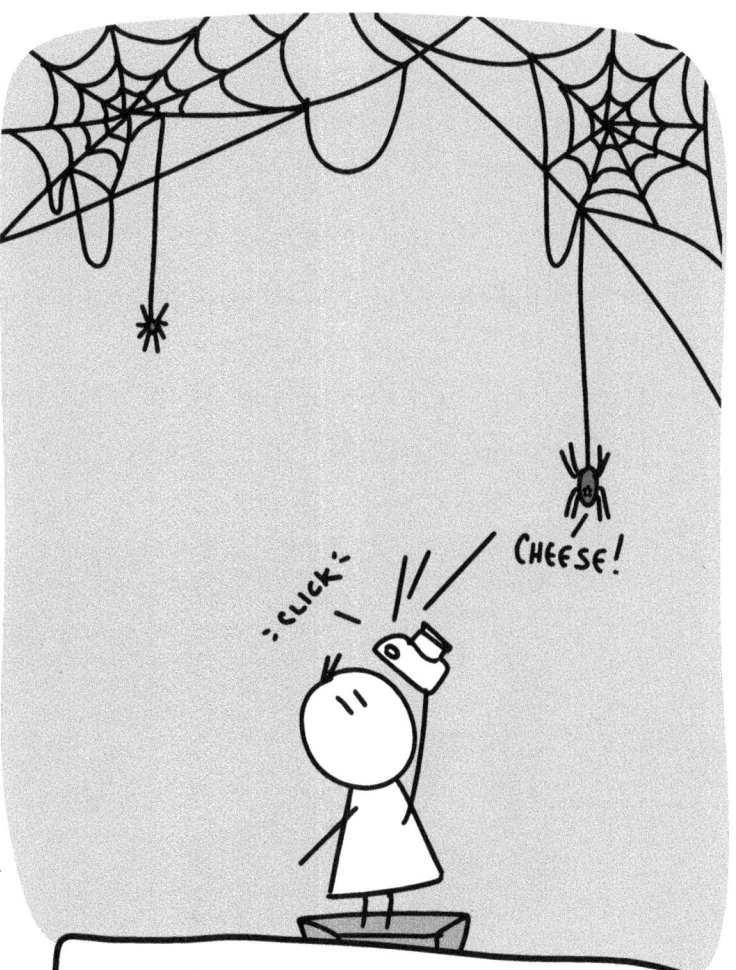

REASONS WHY SPIDERS ARE GREAT!
- Spiders eat harmful insects, like mosquitos, flies, and cockroaches, which helps prevent the spread of disease in humans.
- Spiders can help improve the soil of our crops.
- In many parts of the world, spiders are a symbol of good luck and wealth—spiderwebs are even given as gifts!

DARE 42: GO ON A FLASHLIGHT TREASURE HUNT

One of the most common fears that kids have is the fear of the dark. After all, if Worry is going to try to trick you into believing that bad things are around the corner, it has the most convincing stories to tell when you can't see around the corner.

The dark makes everything feel a little more unknown—if it's dark, you can't tell what's in front of you, which gives Worry an opening to tell you all kinds of spooky stories about what is lurking in the shadows (however unlikely those things may be).

Today, de-spookify the dark a bit with a flashlight treasure hunt:

- Have a parent hide 5 to 10 stuffed animals, tokens, or stickers on one floor of the house.
- Turn all the lights off on that floor of the house.
- Turn on your flashlight and see how quickly you can find them all!

It works best to play this game in the evening, but you can make things easier by playing the game with the shades drawn in the afternoon.

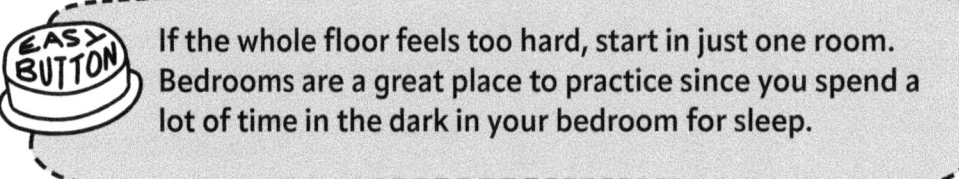

If the whole floor feels too hard, start in just one room. Bedrooms are a great place to practice since you spend a lot of time in the dark in your bedroom for sleep.

DARE 43 · INVITE THE BEES OVER

It's time to get your hands dirty! Let's invite some busy, buzzy friends to a party in your yard.

Get outside and plant a pollinator garden. "Pollinators" are insects that move pollen from one flower to the next, an essential task that allows plants around us to grow. Bees are some of the best pollinators around, and a pollinator garden is a garden with plants that bees like.

Collect a few seeds from one of the plants in the list below and plant them in your backyard or in a flowerpot. A little water and waiting, and you'll have your very own bee show to watch!

- Milkweed
- Catmint
- Bee balm
- Coneflower
- False indigo
- Goldenrod
- Lavender
- Basil
- Parsley
- Sunflower

If tracking down seeds and finding some dirt is not an option, try a trip to a pollinator garden instead! Visit a garden at a nearby school, park, or arboretum, or just walk your neighborhood and ask a neighbor if you can visit their flowers. Stand, admire the busy workers, and see how many different types of bees you can count.

Once you are up close and personal with those bees, remember this:

"IF YOU DON'T BOTHER THEM, THEY WON'T BOTHER YOU."

Chapter 6 · Spooky Stuff (Phobias) · 93

DARE 4.4: WATCH A STORM ROLL IN

Pop some popcorn, grab a blanket, and snuggle in for a spectacular light show! Instead of planting yourself in front of the TV, pull up a chair to the window or go out on a covered porch and watch a storm roll in. Thunderstorms are often associated with spooky stuff like Halloween ("It was a dark and stormy night . . ."), but those flashes are also beautiful! Seeing lightning is like seeing a shooting star—it's rare and exciting. Try making a wish every time you see lightning brighten the sky.

DARE 45 • PET A SNAKE

Super spooky slithering for you today! Visit a reptile store and ask to pet a snake. The staff person can show you around and introduce you to all the scaly residents. While a staff person holds the snake, try taking a few photos (with the employee's permission!) and gently petting those cool scales. After you've met the whole crew, write or draw the types of snakes that you think would win the awards below.

Most friendly	Most beautiful	Most colorful	Most crabby

Most likely to succeed	Most likely to be shedding	Most likely to be class president	Most likely to join the circus

EASY BUTTON: Look at the snakes through the glass instead of petting them.

DOUBLE DARE: Hold a snake!

Chapter 6 • Spooky Stuff (Phobias) • 95

DARE 46: PLAY ALL-HOUSE LIGHTS-OUT HIDE-AND-SEEK

Are you huddled in the dark, all alone, and no one is going to find you?

Perfect.

Or at least, perfect for this Dare: Play a round of all-house lights-out hide-and-seek. Get a group of friends or family together in the evening, just as it's getting dark out. Turn off all the lights in the house and pick one person to be the seeker first. That person counts to 30 while everyone else hides around the now-dark house. At the end of the 30 seconds, they call out "Ready or not, here I come!" and start seeking. As soon as you are found by the seeker, you turn into a seeker as well, until everyone is found.

Playing hide-and-seek in the dark requires a little extra bravery when you're the seeker because you have to get pretty close to a person's hiding spot before you can tell the person is there. You often have to search with your hands as well as your eyes! The dark also means that some places that are not usually good options for hiding are now *really* good options. One time when I played this game, the person who won was hiding *in front of* a TV! They were wearing all black and just blended right in. Good luck and happy hiding!

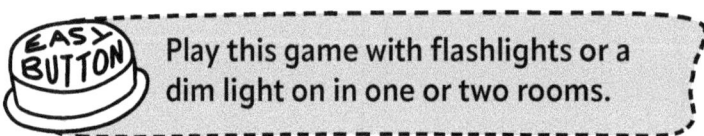

Play this game with flashlights or a dim light on in one or two rooms.

96 • The Be Brave Activity Book

 # GO ON A VERTICAL ENDEAVOR

This Dare is all about reaching new heights. Find a way to get high in the sky, higher than you've ever been before. This could mean you try out being an arborist for a day and climb a tree! Have a parent help pick a good climbing option and venture into the leaves.

Or maybe you decide to find a balcony and pretend to wave to your adoring fans. Jump off the high dive at the pool! Ride an elevator to the top of the tallest building in town and look out some high windows! Climb a ladder with a grown-up spotting you! Try rock climbing at your local gym! Anything to give you the spooky-but-fun feeling of being high in the sky.

Take your pick, but make sure your pick takes you up, up, up!

Struggling with vertical stuff vertigo? Check out the sample ladder for ways to build up to . . . well, UP:

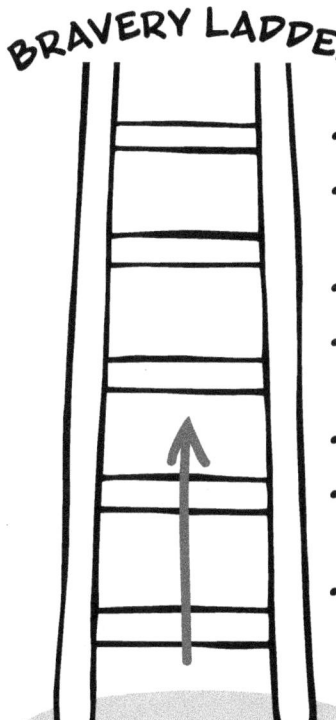

BRAVERY LADDER

- Climb to the top of a ladder with an adult spotter.
- Take an elevator to the top floor of a building and look down from the window.
- Climb four rungs up a ladder with an adult spotter.
- Climb to the top of the school playground equipment and look down over the edge.
- Get on a ladder and go two rungs up.
- Go on a high balcony or hotel atrium and send a paper airplane down to the bottom.
- Stand part way up on a staircase, holding the railing, and notice how high up you are.

Chapter 6 • Spooky Stuff (Phobias) • 97

DARE 48 — FEED A FELINE

Provide a feast for a fancy feline friend: Feed a cat a treat out of your own hand. Get a cat-friendly snack from the pet store or the fridge (mmm, raw fish anyone?), put the treat in the palm of your hand, and hold it out a little in front of the lucky kitty. Give Whiskers a few seconds to approach you and decide if the treat is worth snacking on. Watch out for tickling whiskers and see if you get a lick—cat tongues are scratchy like sandpaper!

 Pet a cat. If you are short on treats or still a little hesitant about offering a snack, give some kitty love and pet three cats at an animal shelter.

DARE 49 — WALK A WAGGING TAIL

Be kind to yet another four-legged friend and take a dog for a walk. Pick a dog that adults have okayed but that still feels just a smidge outside your comfort zone. Maybe this pup is one you don't know well yet or is a little bigger than the others. Grab a leash and a poop bag (sorry)—you are good to go!

 **DOUBLE DARE** Take things one step further and play fetch with a dog. With an unleashed and excited pup running toward you that *really* wants the stick or ball in your hand, remember to stand your ground. If you start yelling or running away, the dog will think you're saying "Play with me! Chase me!" A few slow breaths can help you relax during those first few minutes of play, and once you get used to seeing the pup's enthusiasm, you'll be goofing off right alongside that doggo.

 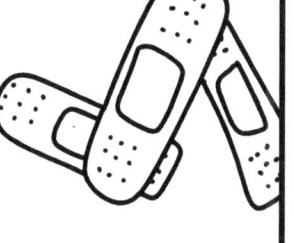

PLAY PATIENT

The doctor is in! One of the most common fears that kids (and adults!) have is a fear of needles. But it's often not just the poke that spooks, it's the whole experience—talking with the nurse, rolling up your sleeve, smelling the alcohol wipe, and feeling the nurse hold your arm during a poke.

For this Dare, get practice with all the parts that go along with the poke by *pretending* to get a shot. Pretend you are visiting the doctor's office for a vaccine today, and have your parent play the role of the nurse. Roll up your sleeve and have your nurse use an alcohol wipe to clean the area, give you a 1-2-3, and then "poke" you with a pretend needle. (The end of a paperclip works well!) After the poke, your nurse will press on your poke spot with a cotton ball and put a bandage on your arm.

 If even a pretend shot feels too spooky, go online and look up videos of other kids getting vaccines. When you search, make sure you search for *"brave kids getting vaccines"* so that you have a chance to witness needle bravery in action!

 Do the real deal. If a pretend shot sounds too easy, ask a parent to check with your doctor to see if you are due for any blood draws or vaccinations. (Flu shot anyone?) Talk to your parents about what a brave visit might look like. For example, a brave visit might be: "I go into the office without help, I sit still and hold out my arm when asked to, and I hold Dad's hand during the vaccine." Nerves and even tears are no big deal, as long as the other boxes are checked. And, most importantly, decide in advance how you will celebrate after a successful visit!

Chapter 6 • Spooky Stuff (Phobias) • 99

SPOOKY BRAVERY BADGE

Check all those boxes?

CONGRATULATIONS! You have earned your Spooky Bravery Badge.

EXTRA CREDIT

Still want more? Try out a few Extra Credit Dares below:

⇨ Write a scary story about your fear.

⇨ Visit a place where you might experience your fear.

⇨ Read a book focused on your fear, whether it's storms, bees, or spiders.

⇨ Watch a video on your fear. (Bee beards, anyone?)

⇨ Throw a Dare party focused on your fear.

CHAPTER 7
Gross Stuff
(Contamination Fears)

It's a classic scene in any horror movie. An unsuspecting person enters a dark room to explore. Groping for the light switch, their hand touches something . . . not so good. Maybe it's sticky, or gooey, or maybe it sort of tickles (and not in a good way). They smell something . . . off. Finally, that unsuspecting person turns on the lights and discovers they are surrounded by . . .

Maybe it's bugs on the wall, or a slimy green ooze that looks extra toxic. Maybe it's crusty, grimy, unknown spots. Maybe it's a glowing red mess next to a warning sign that says "Danger: Radioactive!" This is where gross becomes scary. Meet the very common fear of contamination.

What Are Contamination Fears?

When you have contamination fears, you're afraid of coming into contact with any surface, substance, or item that might harm you. Think toilet seats, a used tissue, or a chemical sprayed in the air. Worry tells you that if you come into contact with that spot on the ground, or you get dirt on your hands, or you inhale that smell in the air, it's going to make you sick—or make you feel so dirty and disgusting that it would be too much to handle.

Contamination fears are common because your brain is wired to try to keep you safe, and sometimes gross stuff really *is* dangerous. For example, you don't want to breathe in the chemical insecticide that an exterminator might use, and you don't want to eat rotting meat. When you encounter things like these that could be contaminated, your brain flashes a warning light that says "Possible danger, yuck! Stay away!"

However, when Worry goes into Eww overdrive, you get a GIANT YUCK reaction for little yuck stuff—the kind of stuff that's a little gross but also necessary and safe, like using a slightly smelly public bathroom when you *really* gotta go. Worry can also start turning on the yuck alarm for everyday stuff that's safe but related to a past gross experience. For example, Worry might tell you to avoid touching your red baseball shirt because that was the shirt you were wearing when you were seven years old and that kid Bob threw up on you at a trampoline park birthday party. (Turns out, secretly scarfing 12 cupcakes under the table right before two hours of jumping up and down was maybe not the BEST idea he ever had.)

Worry's Tricks for Gross Stuff

When you have contamination fears, Worry may trick you into thinking that:

#1 A very bad thing will happen if you do the disgusting thing—even if it's really unlikely.

> If you touch that icky door handle, you'll get dangerous germs on your hands, and they will make you really sick! You'll be in the hospital for days feeling awful with shots and bad-tasting medicine and doctors poking and prodding you and eek!

#2 A gross experience is going to be way worse than it actually is.

> If you pick up the dog poop, you'll get so grossed out that you'll throw up! HUGE DEAL!

#3 You can't handle the feeling of disgust or discomfort that can come with getting sick, even though you've handled it before.

> It would be UNBEARABLE to be sick! You absolutely cannot handle throwing up or feeling bad. You'd totally lose your mind!

WHAT DOES WORRY PREDICT WILL HAPPEN IF YOU GET CONTAMINATED?

Chapter 7 • Gross Stuff (Contamination Fears) • 103

Worry's Demands for Gross Stuff

It's no surprise that Worry's key demand when it comes to contaminated stuff is to avoid physical contact at all costs.

If you *must* touch something gross, Worry might tell you to use a barrier so your skin doesn't actually come in contact with it.

Worry might even tell you to avoid things RELATED to the gross stuff.

Worry will also tell you that if you think you even *maaaybe* came into contact with a contaminant, you must wash or clean it off RIGHT NOW.

Did you touch that spot? I think you might have brushed against it! Drop everything and wash your hands!

Use ALL THE SOAP!

WHAT DOES WORRY TELL YOU TO DO WHEN IT COMES TO THINGS THAT ARE CONTAMINATED?

Why Getting Used to Gross Is Good

Look, people often avoid gross stuff for good reason. It's never a good idea to eat bug-infested roadkill, or to lick a used Kleenex from sick Aunt Mildred. You are smart. You know this. Please don't do these things.

But when Worry is telling you to avoid scary-but-safe gross stuff (public bathrooms!), or things that might have *some* germs on them but are typically "clean enough" (doorknobs! light switches!), or things that are safe when used with caution (cleaning supplies!) . . . that's when avoidance becomes a trap.

Here's a surprise: Even though germs can make us sick, everyone actually *needs* to come into contact with *some* germs, because encountering germs and fighting them off is how our immune system learns to protect us! If your body doesn't come in contact with *any* of the small doses of germs that are found on our everyday things, like school supplies or kitchen tables, your immune system will be weak, just like muscles that never get a workout. Then, when those inevitable bigger doses of germs come along ("Thanks for that sneeze in my face, Steve. Just what I wanted while eating my lunch . . ."), your immune system won't be able to fight them off. Hello, sickness.

Everyone also *needs* to get confident doing gross stuff sometimes because "never ever feeling disgusted ever" is unrealistic in a full and fun life. For example, if you plan to live in your own house someday, then you will probably have your own toilet.

> Please, do have a toilet in your house. The alternative is much worse.

At some point, the toilet will clog and overflow. Grown-Up-Adult-You will have to clean it up, and it will be disgusting . . . but also, probably fine. When you can get confident handling gross stuff, these regular gross moments won't stop you in your tracks.

GROSS... BUT ALSO AWESOME

Can you figure out what other fun and important life stuff might sometimes involve moments of grossness? Guess the answer for each gross thing below.

1. I'm a place that kids will *beg* to go to. I have public toilets, lots of smells, and questionable sticky spots on the ground. Crowds of people touch my handrails all day long, and my surfaces are often dirty and smudged. Sometimes kids even throw up after buying my ticket and riding my rides. What am I?

2. I'm someone who people love to snuggle and admire. But if you want to hang out with adorable me, you better be ready to clean up my poop many, many times a day. As thanks for cleaning my bum for me, I'll spit up on you, cry, and maybe even pee or poop on you if you're extra lucky. Who am I?

> Do you think anyone has ever pooped on your parents? You should probably ask them. The answer might surprise you...

3. My job is all about helping others and making people feel better. As part of my job, I work with people who cough, sneeze, and throw up around me... a lot. I have to touch smelly feet, infected skin, and puss-filled blisters, and I have to listen to people tell me all about their bodily functions and grossest body moments. What job do I have?

Answer key: 1. An amusement park, 2. Sweet little babies, 3. A doctor

What to Do Instead

With contaminated stuff, your goal is *not* to make things not gross. After all, poop, germs, and smelly stuff will always equal disgust. Instead, your goal is to practice the feeling of Eww. To feel confident about handling those moments when disgust shows up. To be able to say "Eww" but also "NBD" when asked to clean those crusty, dirty dishes, take out the trash, or help babysit a sick younger sibling.

The Dares that follow are designed to trigger the feeling of Eww so that you can practice handling that feeling, letting it pass on its own, and continuing to live your awesome life despite it.

Chapter 7 • Gross Stuff (Contamination Fears) • 107

Pro Tips: KEEP IN MIND THAT GROSS IS A STICKY FEELING

Contamination worries are not all created equal. For some, avoidance of contamination is driven by fear. Kids with this fear are anxious that they will get sick and die from a contaminant, or that their contamination will lead to a specific feared outcome like throwing up. For this set of kids, interacting with the contaminant in a safe-enough way is the goal until the fear goes away. However, for other kids, avoidance of contamination is driven by disgust. For these kids, the feeling of being grossed out is so uncomfortable, so intolerable, that they believe they'll never recover.

Fear is associated with a part of the brain called the *amygdala*, which primes us to fight back against or run away from perceived threats (a.k.a. the fight-or-flight response). Disgust, on the other hand, is associated with the insula, which takes in information from our senses and alerts the amygdala and other parts of the brain when it registers something that could make us sick. It also files away this information into long-term memory so we can avoid disease in the future.

Why does this matter? When it comes to exposures, the difference between amygdala-based fears and insula-based disgust is a big one, because while the amygdala can make speedy adaptations to its threat assessment when it receives information that suggests safety, the insula is not as quick to change its interpretation about whether or not something will make us sick. Rotting meat or feces are pretty much always associated with disease, so our brains don't really change the disgust reaction we have to them, even if they didn't make us sick this time around.

This means that with practice, contamination *fears* will reduce over time. The scary thing will usually stop being so scary. But with *disgust*, the gross thing will . . . usually continue to trigger disgust.

Since disgust is such a sticky feeling, you need to manage your expectations for the Dares in this category if your child's avoidance behaviors are driven by disgust. While repeated exposure to disgusting things can "soften" the disgust reaction over time, it's unlikely that the feeling will go away completely. Consider a doctor who treats foot infections: No matter how many times they see it, a smelly infected foot will probably always be objectively gross. But, over a 20-year career, the doctor may no longer have a strong disgust reaction every time he has to treat a foot covered in fungus. The disgust becomes easier for that doctor to shrug at and move past.

With this in mind, the goal for these kids is not to *get rid of* disgust but, rather, to *get used to* disgust so the feeling itself isn't feared or excessively avoided. Here are a few ways that you can help kids move in the brave direction with disgust:

- **Relax into disgust:** When we are grossed out, our bodies tense and our breathing becomes shallow or nonexistent, which only makes the feeling worse. Coach your child to relax into the feeling of disgust by unclenching their stomach muscles and relaxing the muscles in their shoulders, face, and jaw. Taking one to two slow breaths can also help. (Make sure to have them breathe through their mouth if there's a smelly situation that's triggering the grossed out feeling.)

- **Model that you can handle Eww:** Disgust sensitivity has a genetic component, so if you are yuck-sensitive, chances are good that your child will be too. This sensitivity can snowball if you model avoidance and other safety behaviors, which your kid then proceeds to copy. Where did they first see that use-a-shirtsleeve-to-open-door trick? Show your child that disgust is handleable by being just cautious enough when tackling gross tasks. Think cleaning gloves and paper towels instead of hazmat suit and gas mask when cleaning up your dog's stinky little accident on the carpet.

Gross Stuff: Dares

DARE 51: MAKE FAKE VOMIT

Part cooking project, part science experiment: Mix and match ingredients from your kitchen to create fake vomit. Start with the base recipe below and mix in whatever ingredients you have on hand that you think will amp up the ick factor. If you take on this Dare with others, make a competition out of it! The most realistic looking and smelling vomit wins.

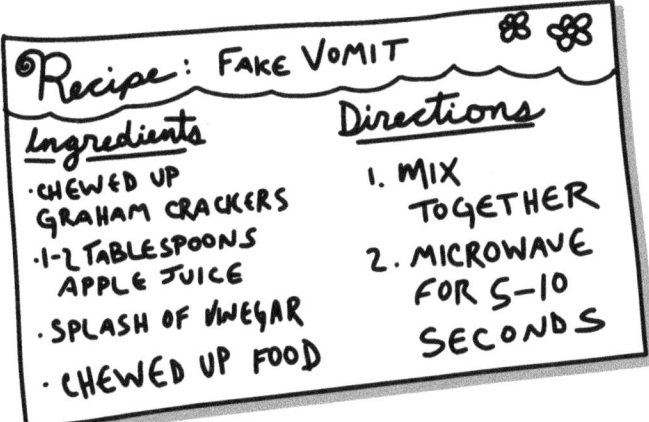

Feel free to add other ingredients to change the color, texture, and smell of your "vomit." Options might include:

- Cream of mushroom soup
- Oatmeal
- Milk
- Orange juice
- Sour cream
- Creamed corn
- Gelatin
- Torn bread
- Pickle juice
- Relish
- Mushed beans
- Whatever your heart desires!

DOUBLE DARE: Put the mixture in a cup and pretend to throw up into a garbage can.

Chapter 7 • **Gross Stuff (Contamination Fears)** • 109

CLEAN THE TOILET

Today's the day to assist your parents with their least favorite chore: Help clean the toilet in your house. Have your parents show you what cleaning products to use and how to use them. Then get to scrubbing!

 **EASY BUTTON** Stick to cleaning just the outside of the toilet.

 **DOUBLE DARE** After cleaning it, eat an M&M that touched the toilet lid or seat.

GET DIRTY

If "a little dirt never hurt," then a lot of dirt shouldn't be a big deal either, right? Embrace your inner piggie and squish, squelch, or dig in a pile of mud. Make a mud castle, make mud angels, squish it like slime, or throw a mud ball as far as you can. Jumping up and down in muddy puddles, anyone?

 **EASY BUTTON** Use only your hands and keep the digging contained to a planter or bucket.

 **DOUBLE DARE** After getting all muddy, have a picnic *in* the mud, complete with a dirt dessert: chocolate pudding with crumbled chocolate cookies on top, and a gummy worm poking out. No washing up first!

DARE 54) PLAY MYSTERY SPOT TAG

Have a parent go around your house and take photos of 5 to 10 questionable-looking mystery spots on the walls, carpets, or furniture. Is that a dribble of old coffee grounds or a smear of grime from your soccer cleats? A speck of your little brother's snot or perhaps a splotch of old cat pee? A melted and redried piece of candy or the poop of an itty-bitty unicorn? Who knows! Whatever it is, your job is to hunt for and find each of those mystery spots and to tag them with your bare hand.

Before you start, guess how long it will take you to find and tag all the spots, then see if you can beat your time. Better yet, try this Dare with a friend or sibling and compete against each other. Who can complete the challenge first?

PARENTS: Take photos from a slight distance to provide some context clues, or play "Hot-Cold" to let kids know if they are getting "warmer" when searching. If it proves too hard to find the spots without additional clues, you can put a sticker close to each spot you've photographed. Kids can collect the stickers once they touch the spot.

DOUBLE DARE: Reverse-wash your hands after touching each spot. Rub your hands together as if you're washing your hands in order to evenly "spread" that contaminant.

Chapter 7 • Gross Stuff (Contamination Fears) • 111

 # PLAY A CONTAMINATED CARD GAME

Go from Joker to the King of Poker Faces with this Dare: Play a contaminated card game.

Take a deck of cards and get them *juuust* dirty enough. Touch the card faces to the bathroom floor or to a few well-used door handles. Maybe take a few special cards and rub them on that weird brown spot under the table that you don't really want to know about. You want the cards to be gross enough that playing with them feels a little Eww, but not so messed up that the cards are truly ruined.

Then shuffle well, deal a hand, and play! Solitaire or Memory Match are great options if you're playing solo. Once you start adding other players, the options are endless—Go Fish, War, Spit/Speed, Uno—your choice!

This Dare is also great for working your way up to trickier levels of contamination. Check out the ladder below for an example of how to build up to Eww. For each ladder item, (1) contaminate, (2) shuffle, and (3) play:

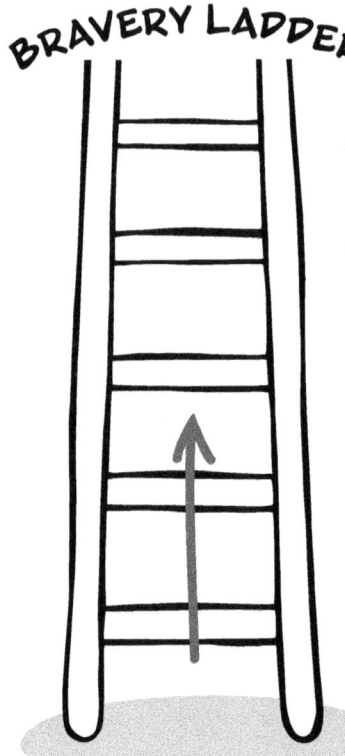

- Take the entire deck and play 52-Card Pickup on a contaminated surface (like the bathroom floor).
- Take all the red cards and put them in a bowl, then "toss" them with a gross contaminant.
- Touch all the face cards (front and back) to a moderately contaminated thing (like the outside of a garbage can).
- Take all the Aces and set them on the bottom of a shoe for five seconds.
- Touch the edge of one card to a mildly contaminated thing (like an unwashed sock).

GO ON A POOP SCAVENGER HUNT

Get ready to be a party pooper, because today, the poop *is* the party. That's right, it's time to head out on a poop scavenger hunt.

Like a treasure hunt for brown jewels, take a walk around your neighborhood in search of animal scat. *Scat*, another word for animal poop or droppings, can tell you what kind of animals are wandering your neighborhood, what they've been eating, and where they've been foraging or hunting. Set a timer for 30 minutes and see how many types of poop you can find, photograph, and identify. Turn the page for a *Poop Guidebook* to help you with this Dare.

DRAW OR MAKE NOTES ABOUT YOUR POOP DISCOVERIES BELOW!

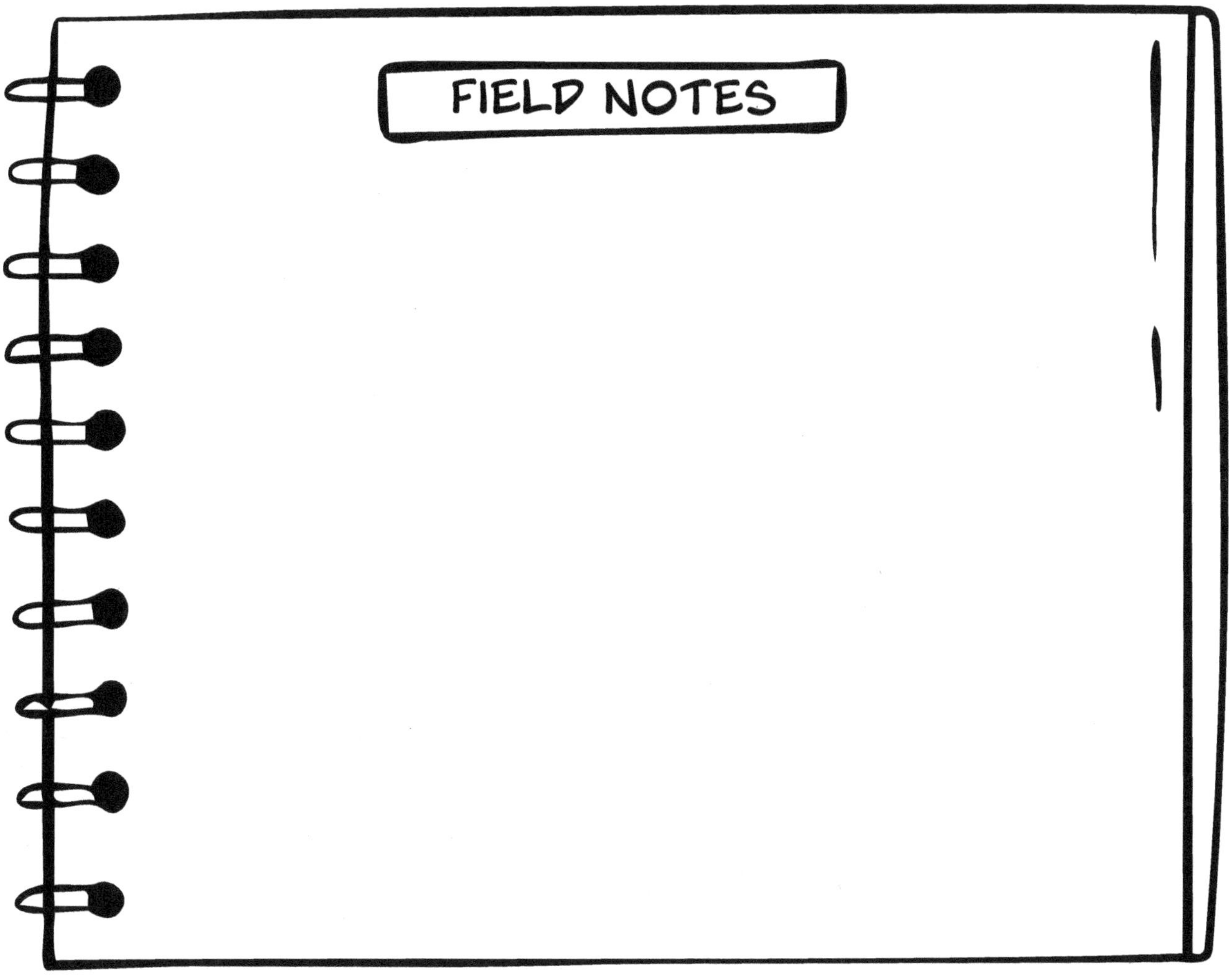

FIELD NOTES

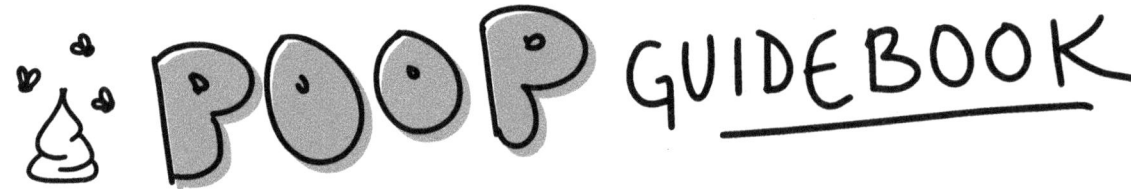 # POOP GUIDEBOOK

In most neighborhoods, you might come across . . .

DOG SCAT: Dog poop is often cylinder shaped and lumpy or segmented, with a mushy texture. It can vary in color depending on the dog's diet, but it's commonly brown.

CAT SCAT: Cat poop is usually small and cylinder shaped, like pellets. It's often dark brown or black and can sometimes look shiny due to its moisture content.

RACCOON SCAT: Raccoon scat is tube shaped and typically dark brown or black in color, with undigested food like berries or seeds visible. It often has a strong, musky odor.

SQUIRREL SCAT: Squirrel droppings are small and oval shaped, resembling rice grains. They are usually brown or black and can be found around the base of trees or wherever there's a squirrel party.

BIRD SCAT: Bird droppings vary widely depending on the species but are generally whitish or grayish in color with a creamy or pasty texture.

RABBIT SCAT: Rabbit droppings are small, round pellets resembling peas. They are typically brown or dark brown in color and may have a slightly tapered end. Rabbit scat is often found in clusters, as rabbits tend to leave their droppings in specific areas known as latrines.

 Scoop the poop! Bring poop bags and collect samples of all the scat you come across.

 ## MAKE A BLOODY MESS

Why wait until Halloween to get a little gory? Make like Dracula-turned-makeup-artist with this Dare and create some gross fake blood.

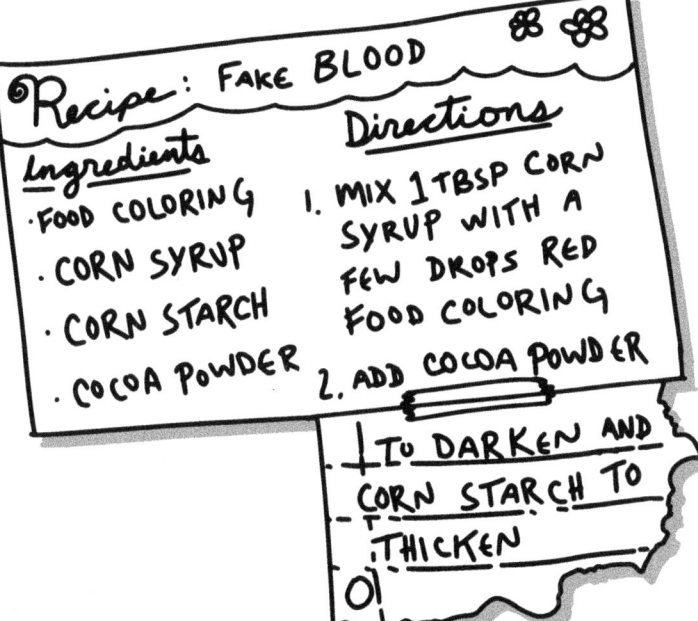

Go ahead and drip some into a toilet, in a sink, on an old rag, down your arm . . . just remember that food coloring, well, colors things. It may not come off easily, so no dripping on the nice furniture or anything you care lots about, and maybe don't cover your face in fake blood right before school picture day (unless you're planning on a very specific vibe for this year's yearbook photo).

 Create a fake wound for your fake blood. Mix cornstarch with Vaseline, adding more cornstarch until you have a putty that is no longer sticky. Add cocoa powder until you think the color is close to your skin, then apply and shape your fake skin into the desired ouchie. Add a dribble of fake blood down the middle and get ready to send any nearby doctors into emergency response mode.

Chapter 7 • Gross Stuff (Contamination Fears) • 115

 ## HAVE A BUG RELAY RACE

Provide some creepy crawly critters with deluxe transportation. To complete this Dare, you'll need three different kinds of bugs that are safe to hold (no bees, please). Lots of lovely bugs can be found in most backyards, but if finding critters in the wild seems tricky, feel free to swing by a bait shop or pet store where you can buy all kinds of bugs. Earthworms, mealworms, and crickets are often available as food for reptiles and birds.

Place each bug in a cup or jar, then place the bug jars in different parts of your yard, at least 20 feet apart, with an empty jar next to each. (You'll need a total of six jars.) You should have a giant triangle of bugs: the Bugmuda Triangle!

You are now ready to Ready . . . Set . . . Go! Pick up the first bug *with your bare hands* and transport it to the next empty jar. Once you've plopped Bella Beetle inside her new home, place Marty Mealworm into your palm and do the same thing, transporting him to the next jar. When you are all done, you should have three bugs in three brand-new jar homes.

Also, you should definitely name the bugs.

Try timing yourself and see how fast you can complete this challenge, or add even more bugs and make this a full-yard event. Go wild!

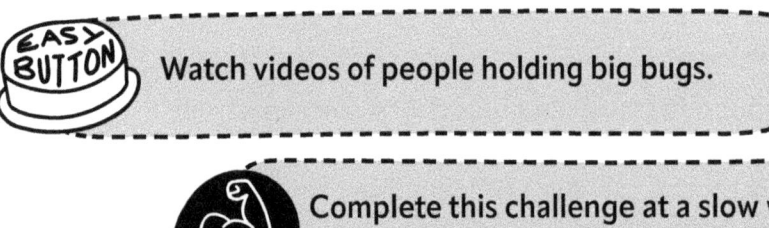

- **EASY BUTTON:** Watch videos of people holding big bugs.
- **DOUBLE DARE:** Complete this challenge at a slow walking pace, with a straight face, and without squealing or dropping any bugs.

Not squealing is the hardest part!

 ## HOST A PUKE SOUNDS CONTEST

Gather your friends and family and host a puke sounds contest. Unleash that inner stomach bug energy and imitate the sound of retching, gagging, and heaving—the best pretend puker wins! Each player gets five attempts, five seconds each, to gross out judges and spectators alike with pretend vomiting sounds. Rate each attempt on a 1–10 scale, with 10 as the most stomach-churning. The person with the most points after all five attempts is crowned Spew Sound Artist of the day. Additional awards of honor go to single grossest attempt and most realistic attempt.

For added pizzazz, this Dare can be combined with Dare 51: Make some fake vomit and pretend to throw up into a garbage can or toilet during your contest.

 Actually trigger your gag reflex during this competition by using a popsicle stick or tongue depressor to touch toward the back of your tongue.

 ## PRACTICE BRAVE EATING

Take yourself on an edible adventure and try eating a few foods that are not (yet?!) your favorite. Try a bite of each of the foods below—a bite means a mouthful, chewed and swallowed. Or make your own challenge food list, including foods with flavors you're not so sure about, or foods with funny textures. Pick five to six foods and be the taste tester you were born to be!

Double Dare: Complete this challenge blindfolded.

GROSS BRAVERY BADGE

Check all those DONE! boxes?

CONGRATULATIONS! You have earned your **Gross Bravery Badge**.

EXTRA CREDIT

Still want more? Try out a few Extra Credit Dares below:

⇨ Touch a public handrail or doorknob.

⇨ Take the garbage out to the dumpster and wait five minutes before washing your hands.

⇨ Clear everyone's plate off the table after mealtime.

⇨ Pick an object up from off the street.

⇨ Pick up after a dog when they poop.

CHAPTER 8
Imagination Gone Wild (Intrusive Thoughts)

The brain can create the most amazing stories and images, cooler and more beautiful than anything you have ever seen in real life. This is the magic of imagination: The only limits to what you come up with in your mind are the limits of your own creativity.

Want to escape from your boring desk with all that homework?

You can think yourself away to a tropical island with a glowing turquoise sea, swaying palm trees, a hammock strung between them, and a hot cheese pizza sitting on the table at its side. Or maybe you're feeling adventurous enough that your mind spirits you off to a bamboo treehouse in the jungle that sits along the banks of a bubbling stream. In the treehouse, you are sitting on a swing, surrounded by seven silly river otters that are ready to party. They jump off the treehouse diving board into the stream while you drink a glass of fresh squeezed orange juice and snuggle the golden retriever puppy sleeping in your lap. Ah . . .

• 120 •

However, those brain-generated stories and images aren't always beautiful, and they aren't always welcome. Sometimes, the brain offers up pictures and stories that are exactly the opposite of what you'd like: dark and spooky, cringe-inducing, or even downright horrifying. You may start out thinking of that treehouse with the diving otters and the sleeping puppy . . . but all of a sudden, your brain wakes the puppy up—and its eyes are glowing red! And its teeth are razor sharp! That devil-puppy starts to growl . . . EEK!

As with any powerful tool, the imagination can be used for good or for evil, and sometimes it can seem like your brain is an evil villain who has decided it wants to scare the pants off you. When those unwelcome mental moments force their way onto the stage, they go by their stage name: intrusive thoughts.

What Are Intrusive Thoughts?

Intrusive thoughts are the uncomfortable and unwanted thoughts and images that pop into your brain without warning or invitation. They are the thoughts you never asked for and that you wish would go away. But, like a zombie in a low-budget horror movie, these thoughts keep popping up again and again when you least expect them and when it's most annoying. They just. Won't. Stay. Down.

Intrusive thoughts can be about anything, but most often they have to do with situations that cause uncomfortable feelings to show up, like . . .

- The thought of a car crashing into yours while driving along the highway
- A scene of you freezing up during your speech, right as you start talking in front of the class
- A story about something bad happening to someone you love that is very unlikely (but technically possible)
- A picture of the disgusting rotting meat that you saw in science class
- The terrifying image of a clown that you saw one time on YouTube and that you wish you could unsee
- A replay of an embarrassing event that happened in the past, like when you told a joke to some kids and no one laughed

WHAT THOUGHTS OR PICTURES HAVE BOTHERED YOU LATELY?

For some kids, just writing down these thoughts can be pretty tricky and takes some serious bravery. If that's you, try reading the rest of this chapter first, then come back to this page. You got this!

Worry's Tricks for Intrusive Thoughts

With most intrusive thoughts, Worry tells you a story that's really horrible but very, very unlikely to happen—it might even be impossible! For example, it might say that your stuffed animal will come alive and follow you to school to mock you about your math test grade.

Come on, a B minus? Do you even know what math is?

However, the main thing that Worry would like you to believe when it comes to these tales of terror is that the thoughts are JUST TOO MUCH TO HANDLE!

Worry might say that if you have an intrusive thought . . .

You'll never fall asleep with something this terrible on your mind!

You'll never be able to concentrate on your homework with this awful image in your brain!

You can't possibly have fun if your mind is focused on this horrible story!

Or even . . .

If you think this thought, you might make it real! It might actually come true!

Worry might also try to convince you that thinking a thought means you agree with that thought, or that thinking about something is basically the same as doing it.

Thinking bad thoughts is BAD! Only bad people have thoughts like those.

Oh no. If you think an awful thought like that, you must mean it! You want that bad thing to happen?! What's wrong with you?!

Chapter 8 • Imagination Gone Wild (Intrusive Thoughts) • 123

Adding to the confusion, those bad or scary thoughts actually get your body all revved up the same way the actual situation would, so when you think the scary thought, it *feels* like that horrifying scenario is happening IRL, right now.

WHAT DOES WORRY TRY TO CONVINCE YOU WILL HAPPEN IF YOU HAVE AN UNWANTED THOUGHT?

Worry's Demands for Intrusive Thoughts

Worry will follow up those comments by telling you that it's essential you do two things:

 Never, ever think the scary thoughts. EVER.

In order to guarantee that those thoughts stay out of your brain, Worry tells you to avoid anything that might trigger the scary thoughts.

What if your spooky thought is about a clown?

And if you do think the scary thought on accident . . .

(#2) You must force the scary thought out of your mind as soon as it shows up.

When that clown image pops into your brain, even with no circus visits, no movies, and no red shirts in sight . . .

Worry will tell you to keep that thought out of your mind with all your might, and to keep an eye out at all times for the possibility that the thought might be trying to sneak back into your awareness. At first, this seems like a great call. After all, you don't want the thought, so you try to get it gone and keep it gone. But it's not that simple.

Chapter 8 • **Imagination Gone Wild (Intrusive Thoughts)** • 125

Why Pushing Thoughts Away Is a Bad Idea

The trouble with forcing intrusive thoughts out of your mind is that it's sort of like pushing them into a sling shot. When you try to keep the bad thought away by thinking of something else (APPLES!), and you put all your focus into thinking that different thought (APPLESAPPLESAPPLESAPPLES), you can keep the thought away . . . for now.

However, the second you let your guard down, the *moment* you relax, that thought will come whooshing back into your mind, and it might even hit you harder.

This brings us to an important fact:

YOU CAN'T CONTROL THOUGHTS, NO MATTER HOW HARD YOU TRY.

In fact, trying to control your thoughts can make them show up more often and make them "stickier" so that they hang around in your mind for longer.

As an example, try this experiment: On the count of three, don't think of a pink elephant for a full minute. You can think about anything else, but keep those thoughts of pink elephants out of your mind. No thoughts of them dancing in a field of daisies, or snuffling you with their trunk, or swishing their adorable pink tails. Ready? 1-2-3, GO!

How did that work out for you?

Umm, for me, not so great.

If you're like other kids, then this was not easy. In fact, even though you probably aren't all that interested in pink elephants, as soon as you tried not to think about them, all of a sudden those big-eared rosy giants were barging into your mind.

Here's why: In order to remember to NOT think about a pink elephant, you HAVE to think about that pink elephant. Tricky, right?

On top of that, if you panic every time an intrusive thought shows up, you train your brain to treat those intrusive thoughts as important and dangerous (even if they're not). Your brain starts to react to those thoughts as if they're an emergency, sounding the alarm every time one shows up.

Chapter 8 • Imagination Gone Wild (Intrusive Thoughts) • 127

Your brain also goes on Thought Patrol to monitor for these thoughts so it can prevent them from showing up in the first place. But the problem is you HAVE to think about those thoughts so you can remember which thoughts you're trying to prevent!

Confusing? You bet. The good news is all you need to remember is this: Pushing thoughts away does not work and does not help. It's also not necessary. Because . . .

Intrusive Thoughts are NOT DANGEROUS

Intrusive thoughts are . . . just thoughts. No matter what Worry says, thinking something does not make it true. If it did, I could think my way to being an instant billionaire, or to having green skin and glitter hair. In fact . . .

Intrusive Thoughts are NORMAL

Everyone has unwanted stories and images that pop into their brains and make them shudder to think about. The human brain is always trying to anticipate bad stuff, new scenarios, and problems that could occur . . . the keyword here being *could*. Thinking a thought does not mean that you agree with the thought or that you want that thing to happen IRL.

What to Do Instead

By now you know that giving in to Worry's demands will only make Worry bigger, while doing the opposite will make Worry smaller.

This ends up being true with thoughts too. If Worry demands that you push a sticky thought away, you actually want to do the opposite. That's right: If you want to think a thought less, then think about it more.

Yep. Turns out, letting your brain spend some time on an intrusive thought will actually help your mind get used to it over time. When you face that thought again and again on purpose without trying to push it away, your brain learns that the thought isn't important, isn't an emergency, and isn't linked to bad stuff happening in the real world. Once your brain knows that the thought is no big deal, it stops going on Thought Patrol, and the thought shows up less and less.

Sometimes called *imaginal exposures*, the Dares that follow are all about embracing your inner scary storyteller, leaning into those tales of terror, and giving yourself the chills by trying out different ways of thinking spooky thoughts on purpose.

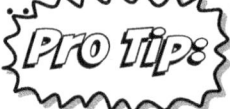 **LIMIT RUMINATION WITH WORRY TIME**

It's easy to get "stuck" on Worry thoughts. Anxiety feels like an emergency in our bodies (it's activating the body's alarm system, after all), and anxious thoughts are great at pulling us in, making it feel like we have to focus on the problem RIGHT NOW. But with a lot of those worries, there is no solution in sight and no way to be certain of safety. Trying to problem-solve Worry can quickly lead us to rehash the same uncertain future again and again. When we're stuck on this hamster wheel of thought, it's called *rumination*.

Rumination is great for exactly one thing: amplifying Worry. When we ruminate, we train our brains to believe that anxious thoughts are urgent and important, needing immediate attention. The brain, trying to be helpful, will then give us even more "what ifs" and "oh nos" throughout the day.

Parents often get roped into their child's rumination. When an oh-so-uncomfortable thought shows up alongside those oh-so-uncomfortable feelings, kids want to feel better FAST. So of course, they turn to you—their brilliant parent, the master fixer who has proven to be a pro at providing comfort. You may start out by offering a few words of reassurance but quickly find yourself sucked into a vortex of "but what about..." questions that can eat up an entire afternoon. What's worse, when rumination really takes hold, you start having to play Whack-A-Mole with Worry as more and more reassurance questions pop up throughout the day. If each question takes 2 minutes to work through (and then 5 minutes, then 15 minutes) and you get five questions a day (and then 10 questions, then 20 questions)... I'm sure I don't need to tell you that it adds up.

Instead of letting Worry suck the whole family in, give your child permission to press pause on their anxiety by setting aside 15 minutes in the late afternoon for Worry Time. If a Worry thought comes up in the day, tell your child to "save it for Worry Time" by writing the thought down and setting it aside. When Worry Time comes around, give your child your undivided attention. Listen to your child, let them know that their worries are understandable and manageable, and refocus your efforts on getting the facts about the situation, then making a plan for the parts of the situation you can control.

The beauty of Worry Time is that it affords children the opportunity to learn that scary thoughts are not a crisis, even if they feel like it, and that anxious feelings don't have to stop them from living their fantastic lives and doing what matters (even if the feelings are still there, right now).

An anxious thought in the middle of a playdate does not mean the playdate has to stop and your child needs to go into emergency response mode. That worried feeling is uncomfortable but not actually paralyzing, and it's also not permanent. Have them write down what Worry is saying and refocus on the playdate, and the anxious feeling will often drift away on its own. Many kids find that when they return to their worries during Worry Time, the scary thoughts feel a lot less urgent and are much easier to challenge.

Intrusive Thoughts: Dares

DARE 61: LISTEN TO A GHOST STORY

Go ahead and get spooked! For this Dare, your job is to listen to a good ghost story. Settle in with a soft blanket around a fire, the logs crackling and shadows dancing around you . . . or, you know, watch a campfire video on YouTube or something. Either way. Get cozy.

Ask a family member or friend to tell you a scary story. If you have a talented tale-inventor on your hands, this story can be made up on the spot. If not, you can find lots of good spooky stories online. If it starts to get a little intense, take a few breaths and look at your surroundings. Worry might tell you to get up and walk away, but remember—it's just pretend! Or is it . . .

 **WRITE THE SCRIPT FOR YOUR OWN HORROR MOVIE**

Lights, camera, action! Create a your very own scary movie script. This film does not need to feature blood and gore. In fact, to make this Dare most helpful, your horror script should focus on one of your own personal fears. Are you afraid of heights? Your script might include a person falling from a high balcony or going rock climbing and slipping. Nervous in social situations? Your script might be about farting in an elevator (yep, loud and smelly) or freezing up during a speech.

Like any good horror film, make sure the ending is sufficiently ominous. This is *not* the movie where everyone lives happily ever after. In fact, this script might end with "and nothing was ever the same again!"

 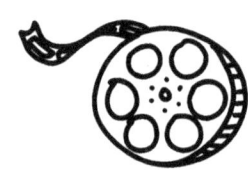 

 Lacking inspiration? Roll the dice or pick a number out of a hat to select your movie's setting and plot. Here are some ideas you can assign each number:

Movie theme: (1) you do something embarrassing, (2) you get hurt, (3) someone else gets hurt, (4) something breaks or lights on fire, (5) something gross happens, (6) something supernatural happens

Movie setting: (1) at school, (2) at home, (3) in the woods, (4) at a friend's house, (5) at a sport practice, (6) at a birthday party

Additional character: (1) cousin, (2) friend, (3) parent, (4) teacher, (5) Dwayne "The Rock" Johnson, (6) Abraham Lincoln

 ## WRITE IT LIKE YOU MEAN IT

Instead of pushing away your scary thoughts, make the thoughts official by writing them down. For the scariest thoughts, you can start by writing the thought as a "what if." For those thoughts that feel easier to handle, try writing them as a possibility ("it might happen that . . .") or a certainty ("today or tonight . . ."). For example:

BRAVE: "What if a bad guy breaks in while I'm asleep and hurts my dog?"

BRAVER: "A bad guy might break in and hurt my dog."

BRAVEST: "Tonight, a bad guy will break in and my dog will get hurt trying to stop him."

 **DARE 64**

PLAN FOR A REAL-WORLD WORRY

Refocus on what is in your control by making a plan for a real-world fear that is possible or even likely to happen at some point. Maybe it's the possibility of severe weather, or maybe it's the possibility that the internet stops working and you can't show a video during a big class presentation. Whatever Worry says will happen, make a specific and realistic plan for what to do in that situation.

For example, are you most worried about what would happen to your dog Fluffy if tornado sirens were to come on? Make sure that your plan includes exactly what you can do to prepare. Practicing the "come" command and having dog treats stocked with your storm supplies might be a good start. Making a plan and taking action provides you with a sense of control and helps you feel confident that even if bad stuff happens, you can handle the outcome.

MY REAL WORLD WORRY:

MY ACTION PLAN:

DARE 65 — DRAW YOUR FEAR

Let that inner artist into the creepy basement of your mind and draw one of your fears. Instead of pushing the scary image away, shine your brain's spotlight on it and bring it to life on a page. Use whatever materials you'd like: pencil, pen, markers, magazine images, mud, even fake blood (see Dare 57 for a recipe). Facing your fears means facing thoughts, preferably in HD. When you take in all their spooky, glorious detail, you quickly learn that nope, thoughts can't hurt you.

The level of detail you put into your drawing will change how challenging this Dare is. See the sample ladder below for ways to move from easy and vague to scarily specific:

BRAVERY LADDER

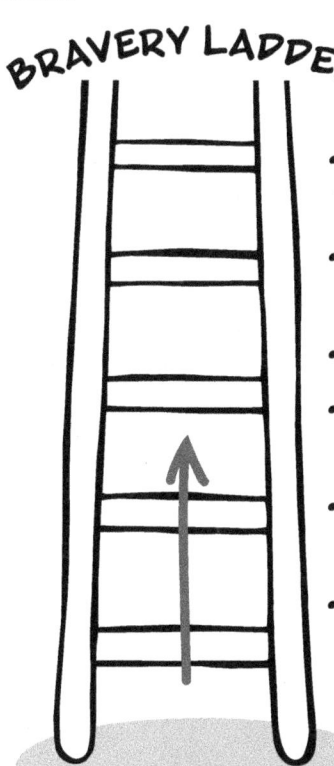

- Create the most detailed and accurate drawing you can. At the bottom, add a written description of what is in the drawing.
- Cut and paste photos of yourself or family members into the drawing of your fear.
- Draw your fear on a big page, in color, using much detail as you can.
- Make a color drawing that emphasizes the bad outcome Worry predicts will happen.
- Draw your fear with specific details that show who is there and what is happening.
- Draw a small drawing of your fear using stick figures and basic shapes in black and white.

 **DOUBLE DARE:** Hang up the picture for a regular reminder of that spooky image and the story that goes with it. Every time you see your fear and roll with it, you de-scarify the thought a bit more.

Chapter 8 • Imagination Gone Wild (Intrusive Thoughts) • 135

 ## MAKE A GOOD WISH AND A BAD WISH

Worry sometimes tries to convince you that you must never think bad thoughts because if you do, it will come true. So *can* you control things with your mind?! Let's find out if telekinesis and manifesting are some of your secret skills.

First, think of a good wish. Maybe you're hoping for school to be canceled this morning, or maybe you'd love to find $20 (or $2,000!). Once you've got your wish picked out, try to get that wish to happen with all your might. Grit your teeth and make those tiny veins pop out in your head because you are wishing SO HARD.

Next, wishing just as hard, wish for something not so good. Maybe you wish that your brother's toy starts on fire, that the bully on your block falls and skins his knee, or that 300 dogs work together to block traffic in front of your school. Channel your inner evil wizard and will that bad thing to happen.

DARE 67 — PLAY A SPOOKY PODCAST ON REPEAT

Is there a scary story that your mind keeps telling you over and over? Maybe a nightmare that shows up every few weeks and is always the same, or a Worry prediction that gets stuck in your brain every time it shows up? Take the scary out of that story by making your very own spooky podcast.

First, write down the scary story in as much detail as you can muster. Then use a voice memo app or another recording software to record yourself telling the story. If you want to get extra creative, give your podcast a name and create some pretend sponsors.

"This episode of the Nina's Nightmares podcast is brought to you by . . . cheese! The smellier the better because you know our dairy air smells great!"

Finally, since even the scariest story stops being scary after you've heard it 50 times, your job is to listen to that podcast over and over and over, until it gets kind of . . . well . . . boring.

EASY BUTTON: Record the story in a silly voice.

DARE 68 — TAKE PART IN THE STICKY THOUGHT CHALLENGE

Remember how if you try not to think about a pink elephant, that pink elephant is suddenly hard NOT to think about?

For this Dare, instead of pushing a thought out of your mind, let's try the opposite and see if you can get a thought to stick in your mind on purpose. Think a spooky thought from the Write It Like You Mean It challenge (Dare 63) and keep that thought front and center in your mind for a full two minutes. No letting your mind drift to anything else. Spooky thoughts only! How hard can it be?

 ## DO SOME JUNK MAIL SORTING

For this Dare, it's time to put on your postal worker hat and sort through your thoughts! Write down 10 to 20 different thoughts on index cards. Each card gets one thought. You can write down the first thoughts that come to mind, but make sure that you end up with a mix of helpful thoughts ("Remember, it's Mom's birthday today! Where did I put that cake?"), unhelpful thoughts ("Ugh, that was dumb. I'm Dumblydore McDumbface"), intrusive Worry thoughts ("What if Mom is in a car accident? With a creepy clown? AHH! Creepy clown!"), and neutral thoughts ("Huh . . . turns out that in Mandarin, a penguin is called a 'business goose.'").

What does that make me, a fart squirrel?

Once you have your cards created, pretend you are a post office worker with a bag full of mail. Each card is a letter, direct from your brain. Your job is to sort the cards into important mail (the kind of letters that you'd want to read and reply to) and junk mail (the kind of letters that are a waste of your time and energy). Go through your cards one by one and sort those thoughts. Helpful thoughts? Those go in the important pile. Worry thoughts that you can't do anything about? Label those as JUNK in big bold letters and set them aside into a junk pile.

See that junk mail pile? When those thoughts show up, remember that junk mail is annoying but harmless. You don't have to open that letter!

 **DOUBLE DARE** For the rest of the day, keep a junk mail thought card in your pocket. Peek at the letter from time to time and practice noticing the thought without trying to solve the thought, fix it, or push it away.

DARE 70: STEP ON A CRACK

A lot of kids believe their thoughts or actions will bring good or bad luck. These beliefs are called *superstitions*. Worry can cause superstitions to run wild and get you to follow all kinds of magical rules that feel scary to break. For example, Worry might say that if you tell a friend "I'm going to ace my math test!" then you should knock on wood to make sure you don't "jinx it." Even though knocking on wood has nothing to do with how well you know fractions, it still feels like something bad might happen if you don't follow this rule.

Well, let's see what happens when you go rogue with those magical demands. Break a superstition rule today! Here are a few options to get you started:

SUPERSTITION: Step on a crack, break your mother's back.
CHALLENGE: Play crack hopscotch and step on *only* cracks on the sidewalk. How far can you get?

SUPERSTITION: Breaking a mirror brings seven years of bad luck.
CHALLENGE: Get a mirror (or many?) from a secondhand store, lay a sheet over it, then break it with a hammer or rock. Paint on the mirror before breaking it to create a unique art piece!

SUPERSTITION: Spilling salt is unlucky.
CHALLENGE: Have a salt shaker dance party and salt the sidewalk to your favorite tunes.

SUPERSTITION: A black cat crossing your path is bad luck.
CHALLENGE: Go to an animal shelter and see if you can cross paths with a sweet black cat. Bonus points if you give the kitty a little love while you are there!

IMAGINATION BRAVERY BADGE

Check all those DONE! boxes?

CONGRATULATIONS! You have earned your **Imagination Bravery Badge**.

EXTRA CREDIT

Still want more? Try out a few Extra Credit Dares below:

⇨ Make a picture book telling your scary thought or story.

⇨ Tape up a reminder of your intrusive thought near your desk for a week.

⇨ Watch a movie with a plot that's similar to your intrusive thought.

⇨ Write a fake news article that tells the story of the bad thing that happened because you ignored Worry's warnings about the intrusive thought.

⇨ Play a game that is focused on intrusive thoughts, like using a Ouija board.

CHAPTER 9
Funny Feelings (Panic)

When most people think of scary stuff, they think of the things described in the other chapters of this book. Things like being embarrassed in front of a large group, failing a test, losing a loved one, or touching something super-duper gross. Sometimes, though, the things that feel the scariest are the things that can happen *inside* of us. Ever heard of the fight-or-flight response?

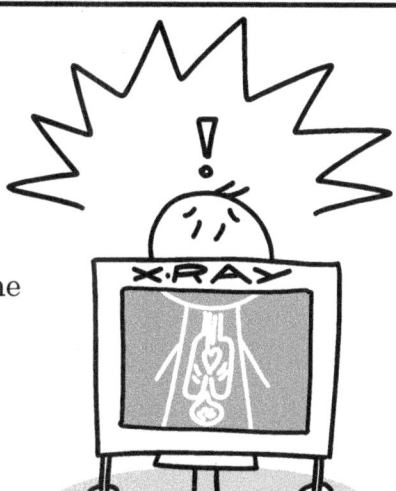

Yes, you have! See chapter 1.

Reminder: Your fight-or-flight response is your body's alarm system, and it can cause you to experience a pounding heart, chest tightness, dizziness, numbness, and lightheadedness. All uncomfortable, but also safe. Although these physical sensations are harmless, Worry can sometimes trick you into thinking that these symptoms will hurt you if they get too strong. It might tell you that your racing heart will turn into a heart attack, that the twinge in your belly means you are about to puke your guts up, and that breathing fast will cause you to faint or even (yikes!) stop breathing at all.

If Worry is making you fear these physical symptoms—so much so that it feels too risky to do anything that even has the *potential* to trigger these symptoms—you might be dealing with panic.

What Is Panic?

Imagine that you are walking through a mall, enjoying a Slurpee and minding your own business, when out of nowhere, your body turns on its alarm system full blast, to DEFCON 1. Your muscles get ultra-tight, with every part of your body tensing. It gets hard to move. You start to breathe faster and faster, maybe even so fast that you start to get dizzy. Your heart races. You get hot and cold all over, your palms are sweating, and you feel like you're gonna barf! You can't think straight, it sounds like you're underwater, and you get tunnel vision until all you can focus on is THIS FEELING LIKE YOU'RE GOING TO TOTALLY LOSE IT AND AHHH!!!

That 10 out of 10 freak-out feeling is panic: a sudden surge in anxiety accompanied by some or all of the physical symptoms of the fight-or-flight response. Panic can occur because of a specific trigger, like giving a speech, but it can also occur out of the blue with no warning at all.

Here are a few common panic feelings. Which ones do you notice the most when that wave of anxiety hits? Color them below.

Worry's Tricks for Panic

While any of the Worry tricks covered in chapter 1 could show up when you're in freak-out mode, the most common Worry trick when it comes to panic is . . .

CATASTROPHIZING: Worry will tell you that strong anxiety is dangerous, when it's really not.

Because Worry tells you to be afraid of the physical feelings associated with the fight-or-flight response, any type of funny body sensation becomes *terrifying*. As soon as you notice any change in your body, Worry jumps in and tells you a worst-case-scenario story about what that funny feeling means.

WORRY MAY TELL YOU THAT:

Worry's Demands for Panic

When you have panic, Worry tries to convince you that even the tiniest change in heart rate or even the smallest gurgle in your stomach must be prevented, because each funny twinge could be the first sign that your body is turning into a runaway feelings train. Your heart will start beating faster and faster, your nausea will get worse and worse, and everything will get more and more intense until BOOM! You faint, puke, go crazy—the feelings are so bad you just can't take it.

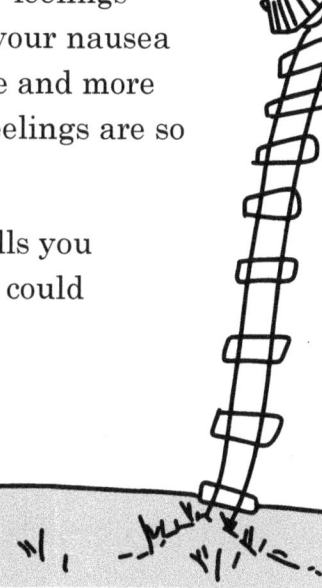

In order to stop this disaster from occurring, Worry tells you (surprise, surprise!) to avoid *at all costs* anything that could trigger panic feelings.

Don't do anything that might make your heart beat fast or make your breathing speed up.

- No running a race
- No jump rope
- No exciting movies
- No dancing

Don't go places where panic attacks have happened before.

- School
- Concerts
- The mall
- Restaurants

Don't do stuff where you're stuck or can't take a break if you feel funny.

- Sitting in a middle seat
- Attending a crowded event
- Going to a movie at a theater

Don't do anything that might make you dizzy or lightheaded.
- No spinning rides
- No trampolines

Don't do anything that might make your stomach feel funny.
- No eating until you're full
- No reading in the car

Safety Behavior Checklist for Panic

Worry will also tell kids to protect themselves from panic by following a set of rules that Worry claims will keep them safe. Which of these rules does Worry tell you to do?

- ☐ Always carry your cell phone
- ☐ Always carry your water bottle
- ☐ Always carry medication to help with panic
- ☐ Don't take medication or other substances that could make you feel funny
- ☐ Always do your relaxation exercises if you feel funny
- ☐ Always breathe slowly when you notice a funny feeling
- ☐ Stay close to exits
- ☐ Don't go places without your parents
- ☐ Don't do activities where you might get hot
- ☐ Always ride in the same seat in a car
- ☐ Never wear scarves or stuff around your throat
- ☐ Always wear your special anti-nausea bracelet
- ☐ Always carry gum, cough drops, or ginger chews
- ☐ Don't eat or drink before doing a risky activity
- ☐ Don't do risky activities for too long
- ☐ Only visit stores at not-so-busy times
- ☐ Don't exercise too hard in gym class
- ☐ Don't travel too far from home or a hospital

Why Avoiding Funny Feelings Makes No Sense

Worry says that if you just avoid panic triggers and keep an extra close eye out for scary sensations, you'll be able to prevent the physical feelings from getting too big to hurt you. However, doing what Worry says is not helpful when it comes to panic, for three reasons:

 WORRY IS LYING ABOUT HOW DANGEROUS THOSE PHYSICAL FEELINGS ARE.

There's no doubt about it. Panic feels scary. Your brain is wired to interpret that racing heart as a sign of major danger because the fight-or-flight response is *supposed* to show up when there's major danger. But in the case of panic, the body's emergency response system has short-circuited, activating the fire alarm when there is no fire. These are False Alarm Feelings, and they are just as safe as a fire drill at school. Annoying? Yes. Dangerous? No.

HERE'S THE TRUTH ABOUT ALL OF THOSE SCARY SENSATIONS:

TRICK OR TRUTH

TRICK: BREATHING HARD = SUFFOCATING	**TRUTH:** Your breathing gets faster so that your lungs can get extra oxygen to your muscles for all that fighting and running you might need to do when you face the danger. Your chest muscles also tighten to get ready for action. Combined, a tight chest and fast breathing can make it feel like it's hard to breathe, even though you are actually getting *more* air than usual.
TRICK: DIZZINESS = FAINTING	**TRUTH:** The fight-or-flight response changes your breathing so that you take in more oxygen (O_2) and breathe out more carbon dioxide (CO_2). The body does this in order to turn you into a marathon runner or super fighter who has the maximum chance of survival against a threat. The extra O_2 or CO_2 might make you feel dizzy and lightheaded, but it does *not* make you faint. Fainting happens when your blood pressure goes down, and when the fight-or-flight response is online, your blood pressure actually goes up!

TRICK:
RACING HEART = HEART ATTACK

TRUTH: Your heart beats faster so that your body can get more oxygen to your muscles for running and fighting. The heart is a super strong muscle and can beat really fast for a long time. Ever run the mile? What about a marathon? That speedy heartbeat can last a long time with no trouble, and it just means the heart is doing its job very well.

A real heart attack usually starts with bad pain in your chest, followed by changes in heartbeat. Heart attack pain gets worse with exercise or movement. With panic, that racing heart shows up first and makes you feel like you want *to move—to run away!*

TRICK:
UPSET STOMACH = GETTING SICK

TRUTH: Your body turns off your digestion when facing danger. Turning food into fuel is hard work, and by hitting the emergency shut-off button on your stomach, there's a ton of extra energy that can supercharge your hard-fighting, fast-running muscles. But, as with any emergency shut-off process, there might be some unintended side effects. In this case, when things grind to a halt, it means you experience nausea and diarrhea.

Stomach, STOP! This is NO TIME to SNACK! ALL FREE ENERGY, REPORT TO MUSCLES!

TRICK:
WEIRD VISION AND HEARING = "GOING CRAZY"

TRUTH: When the brain senses danger, it changes your vision and hearing to try to keep you safe. Your eyes widen and your pupils dilate to let more light in. These changes guarantee you can see the tiger lurking in the bushes, even in the dark, but it makes stuff look weird. Your hearing sharpens and you tune in extra hard to all the sounds around you, noticing more of what's going on. Combined with changes in breathing, this can give people a sense that everything feels weird, fake, or like a dream.

Yep, you're going crazy. Just kidding. Well, maybe you are a little crazy, but if so, it's not from this.

As you can see, those spooky feelings are all designed to help keep you safe, and the body is just doing its job. But those feelings still *feel* dangerous, and Worry still says to watch out for them. This is a problem, because . . .

#2) MONITORING FOR PANIC SENSATIONS GIVES YOU MORE PANIC SENSATIONS OVER TIME.

If you knew that meeting a tiger in the wild was dangerous, you'd keep an eye out for tigers while walking in the woods. Well, Worry says that funny feelings in your body are dangerous, so just like the tiger, Worry demands that you keep watching for those funny feelings so you can spring to action if they show up.

The trouble is, by paying a lot of attention to scary sensations, you end up more sensitive to those same feelings. This happens because when you zoom in and focus your attention on a part of your body, your brain notices. For example, if Worry says that nausea is a big warning sign of a panic attack, Worry will tell you to focus on any and all stomach sensations to make sure you catch the first sign of nausea.

Like a DJ, the brain will turn up the volume on those funny feelings, making you feel the sensations more strongly. As you tune in on those tummy feelings, you start to feel more anxious, which makes you focus on the feelings more, which makes you more anxious—and pretty quickly, a stomach rumble becomes a roar.

FILL IN THE BLANKS BELOW FOR THE BODY FEELINGS THAT WORRY TELLS YOU ARE A PROBLEM:

FUNNY FEELING: _____

BRAIN TURNS UP VOLUME

"OH NO" THOUGHT: _____

FOCUS ON FEELING

As you can see, you end up stuck in a vicious cycle. It seems like you have to stop the feeling from getting any worse, right now! This, it turns out, is the biggest problem of all, because . . .

(#3) TRYING TO CONTROL PANIC FEELINGS IS EXACTLY WHAT MAKES PANIC SHOW UP.

Since Worry has convinced you that funny feelings = emergency, your body turns on its alarm system. Even though you started out with a tummy gurgle that was probably the beginning of a fart (thanks, cafeteria food), you now have ALL the sensations that come in a panic attack starter pack.

These feelings show up automatically and are not under your conscious control. No one can choose to stop shaking on command, or instantly un-dizzify themselves, or decide on a whim to bring their body temperature down to refrigerator-level cold (probably for the best!). Since you can't change these feelings on demand, when you try to control or get rid of those scary sensations, you will fail. This makes you feel even more out of control, and those scary feelings get even scarier. You start to spiral.

What to Do Instead

If you've ever swam in the ocean on a windy day, you know that trying to swim away from the waves doesn't work. You can get sucked under the water and probably get a little tumbled around in the process. Panic is the same: If a wave of panic is coming your way, trying to stop or run away from the feelings can get you stuck panicking for even longer. Instead of running away from panic, you want to face the wave and . . .

. . . float *with* panic instead.

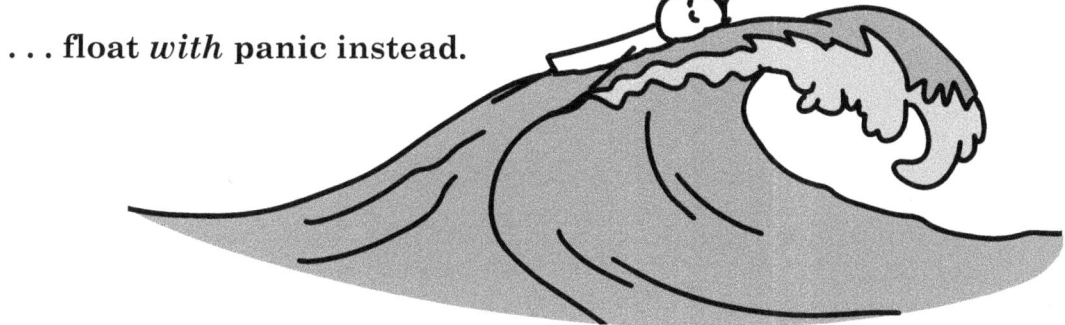

Floating with panic means you keep your body loose and let the feelings pick you up and set you back down without fighting them. When the scary sensations show up . . . you let them be. The feelings might get bigger at first, and they'll definitely be uncomfortable, but they will be temporary.

In order to float with panic, you need to get good at handling all the funny feelings that show up with it. The more confident you are that those feelings are manageable, the easier floating will be. This means your goal is to . . .

⸨ PRACTICE FEELING FUNNY ON PURPOSE! ⸩

The fastest way to quiet Worry about panic is to show Worry that what you're feeling won't hurt you. You can do this by mimicking those uncontrollable spooky sensations with activities that challenge you to get a little silly with your five senses on purpose.

The Dares that follow are called *interoceptive exposures*. Interoception is being aware of what's going on inside your body. These challenges ask you to become a sensation scientist, creating and testing out different feelings and experiences inside your body.

Just like with other fears, if a physical feeling is scary, when you practice sitting with the feeling *on purpose*, it makes the feeling less scary over time, leaving you confident you can handle it when it shows up on its own.

If these Dares seem too easy and you want a little more challenge, double up the Dares and try a few of these sensory experiments at the same time. Combining Dares so that you have two to three funny feelings all at once can mimic panic feelings even better and give you even more confidence about handling those feelings when they show up.

 **DURING PANIC, BE THE SWIM INSTRUCTOR**

The goal during a panic attack is to float with panic feelings and ride the wave, letting the anxiety crest and pass on its own. In order to help kids surf that wave when panic attacks occur, you can channel your inner swim instructor and …

- **Remain calm as the wave is coming:** Help your child see that those feeling waves are safe by using your adult capacity for self-regulation to remain calm in the face of panic. It is much easier for kids to keep it together and re-regulate when everyone around them is already chilled out. A calm adult is also a powerful nonverbal safety signal. It reflects your grown-up assessment of the safety of the situation, which is that these feelings are 100 percent safe and manageable.

- **Don't get out of the water:** Stay put and do not leave the situation, particularly if panic has occurred for your child there in the past. Sticking around is how you can teach the brain that malls, crowds, theaters, and other common panic-inducing situations are actually safe.

- **Call out the wave and remind your swimmer it's time to float:** Instead of trying to reassure your child by saying "You're okay," label these feelings as panic: "This is just those False Alarm Feelings again." Reinforce that there's no need to struggle. The feelings are temporary and will pass on their own.

- **Show how to ride the wave:** Model floating with panic by encouraging your child to watch you and match your (slow) rate of breathing. Regular, slow, steady breathing signals to the brain that all is well. To make sure that floating doesn't turn into mentally checking out and floating away, kids can also "drop anchor" in the present during panic by grounding themselves with their five senses: Have your child name five things they can see, four things they can feel, three things they can hear, two things they can smell, and one thing they can taste.

- **Remind your swimmer to try to enjoy the ride:** While panic is never fun, when your child laser-focuses on the uncomfortable sensations of panic, they are guaranteeing that their experience during panic will be the absolute worst one possible. Like riding a roller coaster with a white-knuckle grip, eyes shut tight, and teeth gritted against the ups and downs, the ride becomes all terror, no fun. Remind your child that despite the uncomfortable sensations, they can experience other stuff during a panic wave too—like the cheer of the crowd during a goal, the joy of spending time with friends or family at a movie, or even the simple beauty of white puffy clouds in the sky. By opening up to the experience and expanding their awareness to include the enjoyable aspects of the moment, you offer your child a path to ride those panic waves with minimum pain and maximum fun.

Panic: Dares

DARE 71: COMPETE IN A STRAW BREATHING RELAY

This Dare takes a little breath work. It might just be the last straw for you . . .

Breathing ONLY through a straw, move 10 little scraps of paper from one room to the next using just your breath. How fast can you do it? Will you try to blow each piece of paper like confetti, or pick up each scrap one at a time by sucking it to the end of the straw?

Compete against a friend and see who can finish first, or guess how long it will take and then try to beat your time. Breathing through a straw can make people feel lightheaded or short of breath—ride the wave of feeling if it shows up and see how long it takes to pass after you've finished the challenge!

DARE 72: GO FOR A WARM-UP JOG

Practice feeling hot and sweaty by going for a literal "warm-up" jog. Run in place or around your yard for three minutes while wearing all your warmest gear: a hoodie or coat, scarf, hat, and gloves. After that bundled bolt, keep those layers on for another 10 minutes and cool off slowly. How long does it take? What parts cool off first?

Chapter 9 • Funny Feelings (Panic) • 155

 ## DARE 73: COMPETE IN THE DIZZY OLYMPICS

Calling all competitors: You've been chosen to represent your country! Or your family! Or do you want to play on behalf of your school? Your stuffies?

Whoever you choose to represent, it's time to compete in the Dizzy Olympics. This activity is best done with at least one other competitor for maximum fun (Mom or Dad, I'm looking at you!). However, no need to stop at two people. Brothers, sisters, friends—for this Dare, the more the merrier.

STEP 1: GET DIZZY!

For 30 seconds before each of the following activities, twirl around as fast as you can. You can put your forehead down on a bat and spin around, get spun in a spinny chair, make like a ballerina and pirouette, or roll down a hill—get dizzy however you like!

STEP 2: COMPETE!

- **Mini Speed Basketball:** The first person to make three baskets wins. (No ball or hoop? Use crumpled newspaper and a waste basket.)

- **Doorknob Dash:** The first person to touch all the doorknobs in the house wins.

- **Target Practice:** Set up five targets around the room. Using a Nerf gun or balled-up paper, each competitor gets two attempts to hit the target—one with eyes open, one with eyes closed. The person to hit the most targets wins.

- **Secret Agent Sneak:** Pretend the floor is lava! Create pillow or paper islands you can hop between as you navigate across the room. For an added challenge, tape string or streamers across your wall and pretend they are lasers so that moving down the hallway starts to take some seriously clever maneuvers. Painter's tape is your friend when setting up a challenge path. The person with the fastest time through the obstacle course wins.

DARE 74. HAVE A BOO DAY

This Dare asks you to make like Scooby-Doo and Shaggy by getting that heart racing with some startle practice! Jump scares, here we come.

Select a day that is Boo Day. On this day, assign your parents the job of surprising you. Their goal is to startle you 5 to 10 times throughout the day, when you least expect it. A good surprise might be popping out from behind a corner (bonus points for doing this while wearing a funny costume), or suddenly playing cheerful loud music when you are sitting in silence. Or of course, they can use an old classic: the whoopee cushion. But parents, be warned: On Boo Day, the Boos go both ways. There is nothing stopping your child from trying to sneak up on you too!

 Watch a series of jump-scare videos or movie scenes on YouTube. Parents, preview the videos first!

DARE 75. WEAR SOMEONE ELSE'S GLASSES

Ever heard of walking a mile in someone else's shoes? Give your feet a break and take your eyes on the adventure instead: Wear someone else's glasses.

For 15 minutes, put on some prescription glasses that are not meant for your eyes. By wearing funny lenses, you get to practice the feeling of the world being "weird" or "off." Things may look fuzzy or warped, and you might feel unbalanced or like everything is a little unreal. Try to notice what funny feelings show up in your body during those 15 minutes and also how long the feelings last after the time is up and you take the glasses off!

 DARE 76 EAT SOMETHING SOUR, SALTY, AND BITTER

Sometimes when your body's alarm system turns on, you can experience a dry mouth and a sour or bitter taste due to the body shutting down digestion and clenching the stomach and throat muscles tight. This Dare challenges you to practice that experience on purpose and see how long it lasts.

Sour, Salty, and Bitter? Sounds like somebody who needs to lighten up...

First, get your mouth all dried up by eating something dry, crunchy, and a little salty. Good options include saltine crackers, pretzels, or dry toast. Next, give yourself a sour and bitter taste by licking or biting a grapefruit (a lemon slice + a drop or two of black coffee also works). After, set a timer and track how strong the taste is minute by minute. See how long you can go without drinking water. Does focusing on the feeling turn the taste volume up or down? Do you notice your mouth watering?

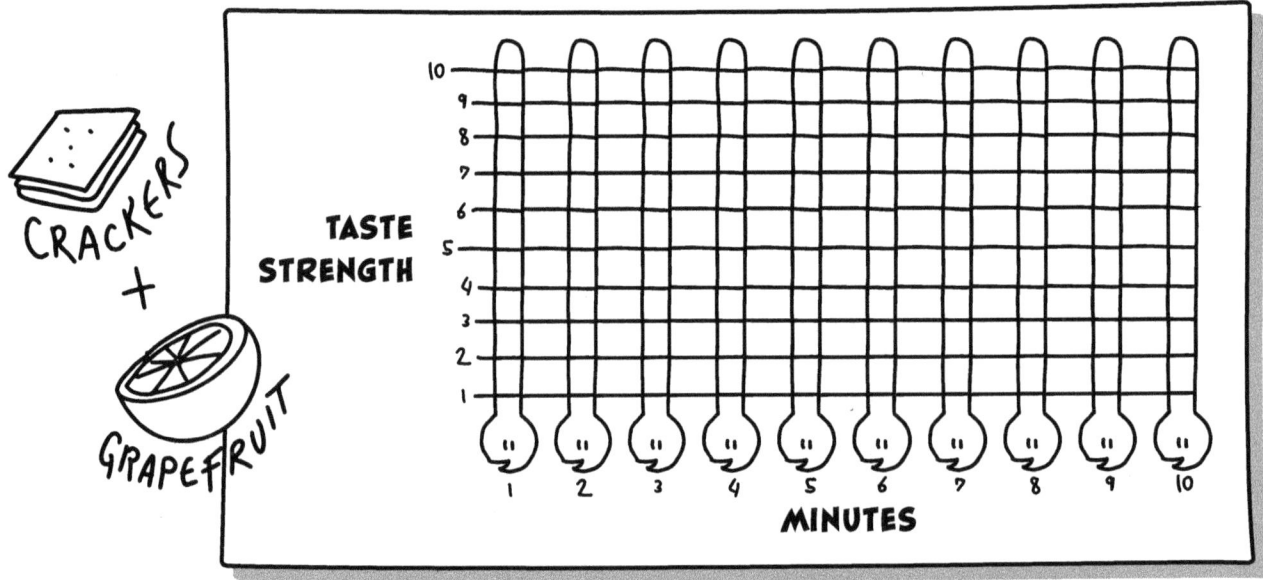

 Try eating a sour-but-sweet candy, such as a Sour Patch Kid, which has a tangy and sour coating over a sweet gummy center.

 After eating something crunchy to dry out your mouth, try an *extremely* sour candy, such as a Warhead! Make it through the lip-puckering moments, and you'll get to a sweet candy underneath, but be warned—this one is eye-watering!

 ## GO UP, UP, UP!

Go straight to the top with this Dare and take the easy way up. Ride an elevator to the top of a tall building. Stand in the back of the elevator to feel just a little more stuck in that windowless box, and notice the funny stomach sensations that riding up and down creates. Try to stay on the elevator for a few trips up and down. The more you ride, the more familiar those sensations will get.

 Just before you arrive at the top floor, jump! If you time it right, you'll feel a little weightless, like an astronaut in space. Remember not to float away . . .

 ## HAVE A SURREAL STARING CONTEST

For this Dare, your goal is to enter into a staring contest that you are guaranteed to lose (um, sorry?). Pick a spot in the room with very little going on—a blank wall or a spot on the ceiling works well—and stare at it until you notice changes in how you see light or patterns. Usually this will occur after one to four minutes of staring.

Like the *Magic Eye* books, when you're staring at one place for a long time, your brain and eyesight adapt to try to detect patterns, and this can change what you perceive. It can also create the sense that things are a little weird or off, like you are in a dream or a different world. Notice these funny changes in sight, see how long they last, and if your vision feels wonky for a while, go ahead and get back to your fun stuff despite the quirks of sight. That sense of "unrealness" does not have to stop you from living your fabulous life.

 Add in some meaningless mumbles. While staring at the wall, say the same word over and over. "Milk milk milk milk . . ." works well. Saying the same word over and over can make the word start to lose its meaning and will add to the sense of wacky world that the staring creates.

Chapter 9 • *Funny Feelings (Panic)* • 159

 JOIN THE BUSY BODIES

Go somewhere that's very busy and full of bodies: Visit a crowded place that takes some effort to leave. The goal is for this outing to be intense and high energy but also fun, so select your outing based on what sounds the most enjoyable. Options include:

In busy places, Worry will tell you to stick to the sidelines and circle around the edge of the crowd, so to make this Dare most effective, your job is to get in the thick of things. Select the middle seat, sit in the middle of a row, go to the center of the pack! With the energy of a crowd, and so many bodies nearby, you'll feel yourself get warm and notice your heart beat a bit faster. It might be loud, and it might feel like you can't move or breathe easily. This is normal—roll with that feeling and see if you can refocus on the fun in front of you!

If crowds are definitely *not* your thing, feel free to work your way up from wide open spaces to condensed chaos with this example Bravery Ladder:

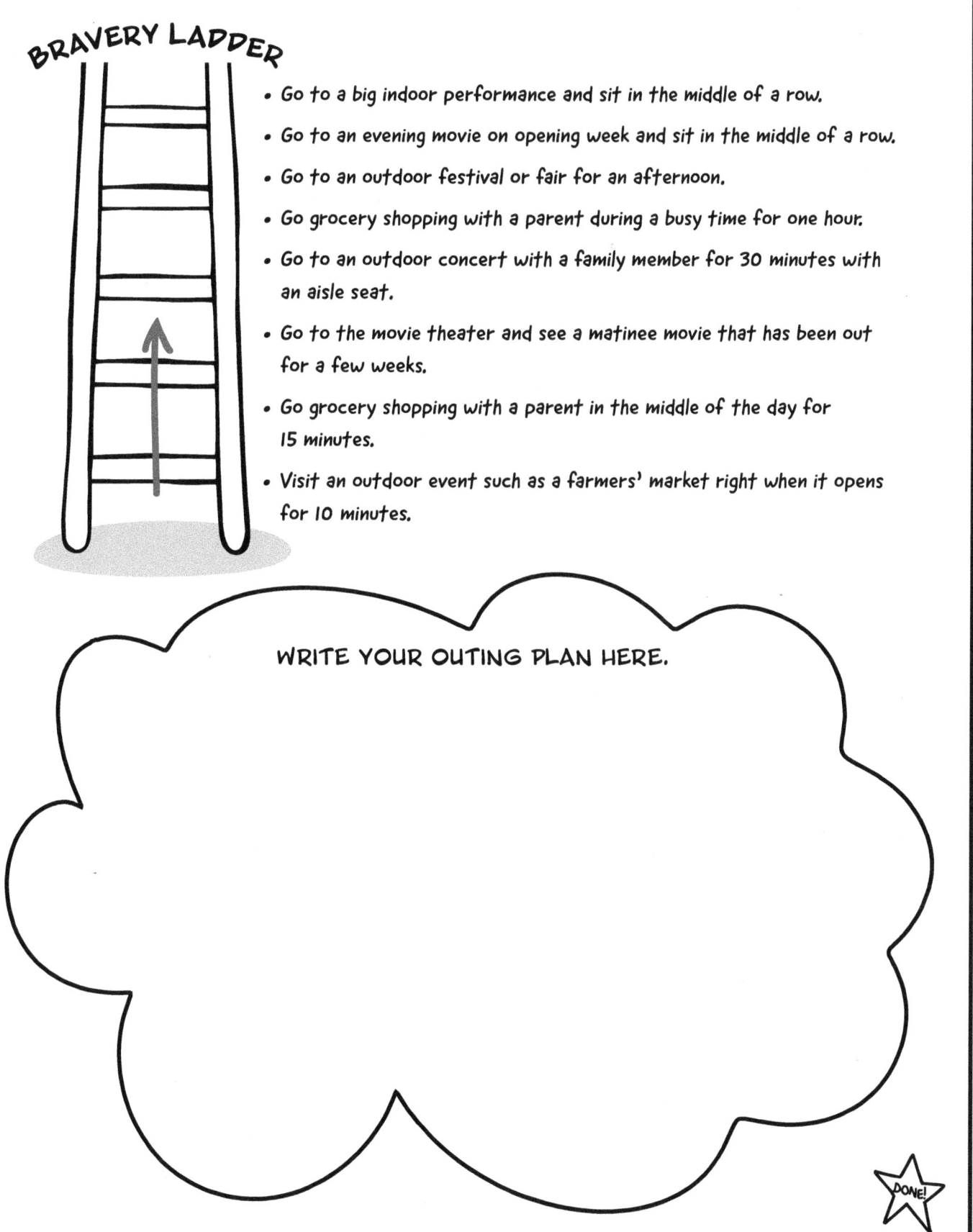

BRAVERY LADDER

- Go to a big indoor performance and sit in the middle of a row.
- Go to an evening movie on opening week and sit in the middle of a row.
- Go to an outdoor festival or fair for an afternoon.
- Go grocery shopping with a parent during a busy time for one hour.
- Go to an outdoor concert with a family member for 30 minutes with an aisle seat.
- Go to the movie theater and see a matinee movie that has been out for a few weeks.
- Go grocery shopping with a parent in the middle of the day for 15 minutes.
- Visit an outdoor event such as a farmers' market right when it opens for 10 minutes.

WRITE YOUR OUTING PLAN HERE.

Chapter 9 • Funny Feelings (Panic) • 161

 ## HAVE SOME AMUSEMENT PARK FUN

Grab a ticket and ride the ride for this Dare: Go on an amusement park ride. Select the ride of your choice, but for maximum effect, pick something that has sudden changes in direction, where you'll get some funky stomach feelings. You can also try strapping into a middle seat to increase the "stuck here" feeling.

If amusement park rides are not an option, you can try any alternate transportation adventure where you're not in control of the stops and starts. Riding on a crowded bus is a great option, or even buckled in a friend's car on the freeway during rush hour.

 Get the feeling of your stomach dropping and heart racing by taking a very big swing! Have someone pull you back as far as they can on the biggest playground swing you can find, and then let go unexpectedly so "eek!" turns to "whee!"

PANIC BRAVERY BADGE

Check all those ⭐ boxes?

CONGRATULATIONS! You have earned your **Panic Bravery Badge**.

EXTRA CREDIT

Still want more? Try out a few Extra Credit Dares below:

⇨ Take a polar plunge: Jump in a very cold pool or bath.

⇨ Listen to a cringey sound, like nails on a chalkboard or the sound of someone chewing, for five minutes. (Check out YouTube—the options are endless!)

⇨ Jump off the high dive at a pool.

⇨ Jump rope with a coat on for two minutes.

⇨ Breathe through a straw while watching a show.

⇨ Trust fall with your family.

CHAPTER 10
Cringey Stuff (Embarrassment)

Ben was already so freaking nervous, and for a really good reason: He was on his very first date. Ever. Ben's mom had dropped him off at the mall, and there he was, in the food court, getting lunch and about to hang out with Cate, the girl he liked! Not just in his head! In PUBLIC!

It was a dream come true, but this dream was about to turn into a nightmare. With a tray full of food in hand, Ben turned and started walking toward Cate's table . . . and . . . slipped.

NONONONONONONO

Everything started to move in slow motion—the soda's ice cubes gleaming as they sloshed out of the cup, the fries turning into giant yellow confetti as they flew through the air. Ben's eyes locked onto Cate's in the very moment that his feet shot out from under him. In a flash, he was on the ground, surrounded by ketchup the very same shade of red as the blush on his cheeks.

Oh. My. Gosh. How was he ever going to live this down?

Poor Ben. His date with Cate included an uninvited guest (and a guest that shows up at most first dates, actually)—say hello to embarrassment.

What Is Embarrassment?

Definitely a top contender for "least favorite emotion," *embarrassment* is the uncomfortable feeling that visits when you do something you think makes you look silly in front of others.

If Worry bothers you about social stuff (see chapter 2), embarrassment might be one of the uncomfortable feelings behind the fear. Instead of simply predicting that others will judge you, Worry takes it one step further and predicts that not only will that kid think you're dumb, ugly, mean, or ridiculous, but their assessment of you will lead you to experience such intense embarrassment that you will want to crawl into a hole and never come out. That horrid, totally mortified feeling is what I like to call . . .

THE CRINGE

The Cringe is a normal feeling, but it's not a particularly fun one. Here are a few examples of cringe-worthy things that have made other kids feel embarrassed. Have any of these happened to you?

- ☐ Tripping in front of a group
- ☐ Missing an easy shot when playing a sport
- ☐ Calling your teacher "Mom"
- ☐ Farting in class
- ☐ Forgetting the words to a song during a performance
- ☐ Spilling food or drink on yourself at the lunch table
- ☐ Mispronouncing a word during a presentation
- ☐ Having food stuck in your teeth
- ☐ Texting a message to the wrong person
- ☐ Blushing when talking to a crush

I'll bet when you read that list, you remembered at least one embarrassing thing you've done.

Write it here:

When you wrote down that memory, did you frown or clench your teeth? Maybe your nose wrinkled or your shoulders tensed up. Maybe you even gave a big ol' shiver and squeezed your eyes shut. Chances are that you got a little taste of The Cringe all over again. This is because when you think about an embarrassing moment, your brain acts like the situation is happening all over again.

Embarrassment's weird cousin is *awkwardness*. Awkwardness is the uncomfortable and self-conscious feeling that you're not quite fitting in with a group, or that something about the way you're acting might be just a little . . . I don't know . . . *off*. Awkward moments leave everyone wincing, wanting to fade into the background or fast-forward time. Like that time when you:

- Ran out of things to say in a conversation
- Made a joke where no one laughed
- Tried to hug someone when they tried to shake your hand
- Accidentally liked an old social media post while scrolling through someone's profile
- Got caught staring at someone
- Tried to high-five someone who did not high-five you back

As uncomfortable as they are, embarrassing and awkward moments are not only normal, they are unavoidable if you're living a full and fun life. Everyone has a good (and awful) story.

True Confessions

Here are some real embarrassing stories from real embarrassed kids.

"I went with my mom and my friend to get a passport for our family trip, and they make you sign your name on it. You can only do it once. I was super excited, and when I went to sign, I wrote my first name with part of my last name. Think 'Janeoeski Doeski.' The passport lady and my friend burst out laughing. My mom, not so much."

"It was a really warm day when we had our end-of-the-year class party, and I was playing Big Base, where you play kickball and run the bases, but you get to stop with other kids on a giant base. Like 10 kids were packed on first base, all sweaty and smelly, and I felt sick. I tried to cover my mouth, but the chocolate milk I had for lunch would not be stopped, and it came out my nose. It was the Puke Sprinkler Party of 2023, and all the kids on base got sprayed."

"Our class was learning about North America, and we were talking about Americans and Canadians. In front of a huge group, I started talking about 'Americans from America, and Canadians from Canaydia.' The room went silent and everyone looked at me funny. I was ready to melt into the floor."

"I called the basketball coach 'Mom' in front of the whole team . . . and it was a male coach."

"We were doing a fitness challenge in gym, and there was a competition to see who could lift this really heavy weight. My friend and I were working together to try to lift it, and I was trying so hard that I farted! It was ridiculously loud and the whole class lost it. I blushed so bad I think my whole body turned red."

Worry's Tricks for Embarrassment

Worry may tell you that doing something embarrassing will cause other kids to refuse to be your friend (unlikely), or it may try to tell you that the awkward moment is a VERY big deal (it's not). However, the most common Worry trick for embarrassment is "unhandleability," or the belief that . . .

YOU CAN'T HANDLE THE CRINGE! That's right, Worry tells you that you could never survive the feelings of embarrassment that come with social mistakes, when the reality is you totally can.

> If you do something embarrassing in front of Bob, you will *never* recover! You will feel the horrible shame of embarrassment every time you see Bob in the hallway, or in class, or at the park, and eventually you will melt into a puddle of awful feelings, never to be seen again. RIP you.

When Worry predicts that something embarrassing might happen in a social situation, it ushers you into the movie theater of your mind and locks the door. Once you're pulled in, Worry starts to play the embarrassing scenario for you on that big mental screen in painful detail—slowing down for the dumbest bits, zooming in on the most awkward parts, and pressing pause at the absolute worst moment, when your humiliation is complete. In that freeze frame, The Cringe feels infinite, and it seems like you will experience the feeling of embarrassment forever.

WHAT DOES WORRY TELL YOU WILL HAPPEN IF YOU SAY OR DO SOMETHING EMBARRASSING?

Chapter 10 • Cringey Stuff (Embarrassment)

Worry's Demands for Embarrassment

In that theater, with the *Very Embarrassed You* movie paused on the big screen at the worst moment, Worry makes its pitch . . .

> The Cringe would be unbearable, and you'd never live it down. You MUST do whatever you can to avoid this awful fate! So . . . don't do ANYTHING that might risk embarrassment!

- No trying something new. What if you mess up?
- No talking to new people. What if you're awkward?
- No telling jokes. What if no one laughs?
- No playing team sports. They might see you miss!
- And especially, DON'T BE DIFFERENT!

Worry says you must look, talk, and act exactly like everyone else so no one has any reason to laugh. Make no embarrassing social mistakes and you'll be *juuust* fine.

Or will you?

Why Trying to Avoid Embarrassment Is Silly

Worry says that if you keep yourself totally average and take zero social risks, you'll be safe from embarrassment. But this is a bad idea, for a few reasons:

#1) IF YOU ARE ALIVE, AVOIDING EMBARRASSMENT IS IMPOSSIBLE.

Embarrassment is a feeling that is unavoidable if you're a living, breathing human being (which you are, right?). Like the weather, embarrassment shows up without warning as a natural reaction to average moments at school, with friends, and in public places. And, as you saw earlier in this chapter, you can experience The Cringe by just *thinking* about something embarrassing that happened to you in the past. It may not be enjoyable, but this feeling is normal, safe, tolerable, and temporary. Which is a really good thing, because . . .

#2) LIFE'S FUN STUFF OFTEN *REQUIRES* EMBRACING EMBARRASSMENT.

There's a lot of hilarity, silliness, and excitement out in the world just waiting for you if you are willing to feel a little embarrassed sometimes. New friends! New sports! New talents! New YOU!

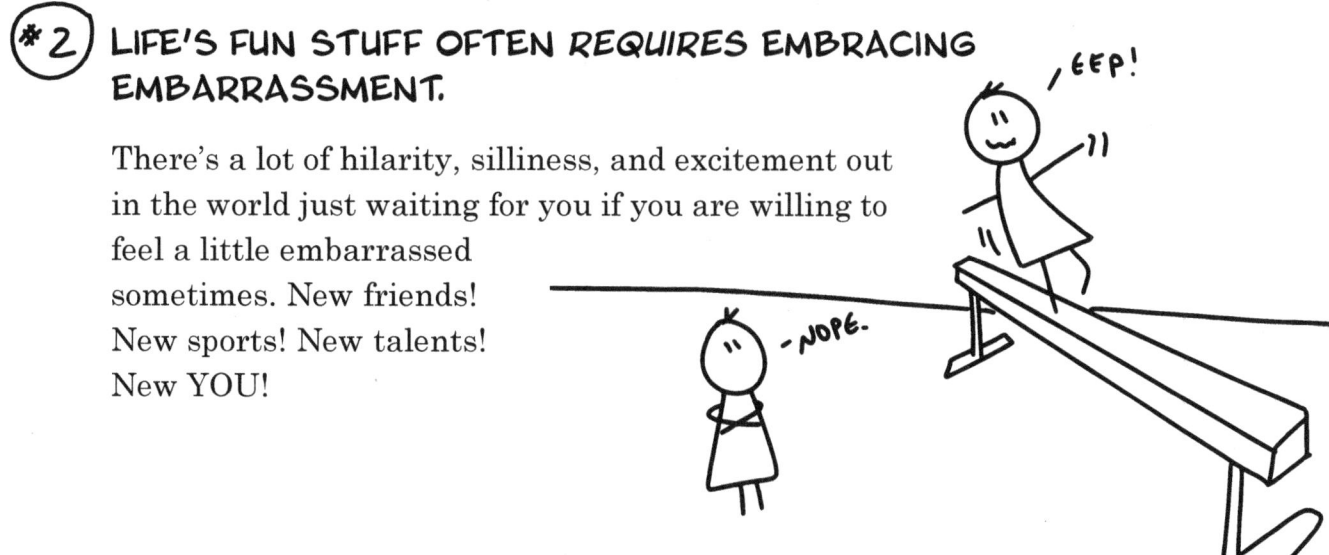

Chapter 10 • Cringey Stuff (Embarrassment) • 171

Anytime you try something new, whether it be learning how to play soccer, hanging out with a new friend, or even trying on a new pair of glasses, you MUST risk the feeling of embarrassment.

Want a new bestie? Making new friends means talking to people you don't know as well (yet!) and sometimes not knowing exactly what to say (or even saying something they might disagree with . . . awkward!).

Want to learn how to play the harmonica? When you try something new, you are a beginner, and beginners goof up sometimes—it's part of learning!

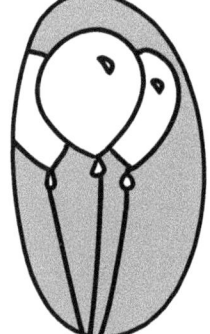

Want to be the life of the party? Getting good at social stuff requires social practice, and social practice means occasional social mistakes.

Want to be hilarious? Being funny means telling jokes, and any stand-up comic will tell you that even the best comedians sometimes miss the mark with their jokes (womp womp).

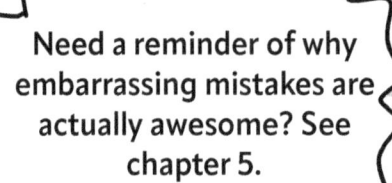

Need a reminder of why embarrassing mistakes are actually awesome? See chapter 5.

What to Do Instead

Embarrassment is inevitable if you plan on hanging out with other people at some point in life. You can wait for those embarrassing moments to happen to you, or you can make them happen on your own terms. Rather than avoiding embarrassment, you want to *master* that feeling. Your goal is to practice The Cringe on purpose so you know the feeling is handleable. That way, when Worry says . . .

Just like with other fears, if you practice embarrassment on purpose, you're less likely to feel scared about The Cringe happening when you can't control it.

ON TO THE DARES!

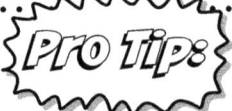

REMEMBER THAT HANDLING TEASING IS A SOCIAL SKILL

The Dares in this chapter are called *social mishap exposures*. These bravery builders are all about breaking social norms and practicing the embarrassing stuff that people hope never happens to them in real life. For example, you may hope that you never accidentally walk around with toilet paper stuck to your shoe. This is understandable. However, if you try out that TP train on purpose, you will get to experience how the feeling of embarrassment is survivable. It comes on, fades, and once the wave is past, you can flush, wash, and move on with your day. What's more, you'll also get a chance to test Worry's prediction and see if the situation actually results in others stopping and laughing, shrugging and moving on, or not noticing at all.

Parents often lament that when kids practice this type of Dare, they are placing themselves at risk of teasing from other kids. The truth is, these Dares *do* risk teasing from others—and that's actually a good thing. For kids to be comfortable in social situations, it's absolutely critical that they gain confidence handling the moments of giggles and teasing that occur when something embarrassing happens.

Navigating teasing *is* a social skill, and like all other social skills, it takes practice. However, practicing for this particular skill can be difficult, because while social mistakes are inevitable during a child's social development, usually those embarrassing moments are unpredictable, leaving no room for prep or planning. What's more, those awkward moments often feel extra scary because they occur at random—your child never knows when The Cringe will strike next.

By helping your child take matters into their own hands and try embarrassing things on purpose, you take the unpredictability out of the equation and give your child a chance to prepare for and try out this skill on their own terms. When teasing shows up during a Dare, they can plan to bounce back from the awkward or embarrassing moment by:

- Keeping it cool with a smile and shrug ("Whoops! Anyway . . .")

- Leaning into it by laughing it off ("Haha, well that's embarrassing . . .")

- Or if the giggles start to get excessive, shutting it down with some assertive talk ("Okay, that's enough teasing for today, thanks.")

And one final note: There is a difference between teasing and bullying. Teasing is typically playful and lighthearted, a gentle ribbing that can actually foster feelings of closeness. Teasing is often done between friends and typically stops as soon as a person says "no more." Bullying, on the other hand, has a hostile tone and is intended as an attack. Bullying comments are purposefully cruel, custom-designed to hurt the victim's feelings. Bullies are also repeat offenders—they do not stop when asked, and in fact may harass a child more if the child is visibly uncomfortable. Kids need practice handling teasing. They do *not* need practice handling bullying. If you believe your child is being bullied, check out www.stopbullying.gov for resources on how to shut it down.

Embarrassment: Dares

DARE 81: ASK A SILLY OR OBVIOUS QUESTION

Ever been called a Silly Sally? Foolish Fred? Ridiculous Rick? Discover your goofball nickname today by asking three people a silly or obvious question. Your job during this Dare is to ask the question in a serious way—no sharing that you are trying a challenge! For the question itself, the sillier the better. Here are some examples to get you started:

- Ask your science teacher, "So what country do unicorns live in?"
- Ask a coffee shop employee, "Do you sell coffee?"
- Ask your coach, "How do you mail a letter?"
- Ask a person standing next to a bathroom, "Where is the bathroom?"
- Ask your classmate, "So how does math work?"
- Ask a kid on the playground, "Have you ever been to the moon?"

Chapter 10 • Cringey Stuff (Embarrassment) • 175

DARE 82: WALK BACKWARD IN A STORE

Take the path less traveled with this Dare: Walk backward through a store. When you walk this way, count how many people notice. Do others laugh and stare, or do they shrug? Do people look your way for one minute, or is it only for one second? How many people seem to care?

 **DOUBLE DARE:** See if you can get people to notice your walk on purpose. Turn your walk silly with some added wiggles and jumps. How hard do you have to work to get others to take notice? Feel free to google "Ministry of Silly Walks" for some inspiration.

DARE 83: WEAR CLOTHES INSIDE OUT

Are you a person who hates the feeling of seams and tags in your clothing? Great news! For today, you won't have to feel any seams or tags, because for this Dare, the inside of clothing becomes the outside! Go on an outing while wearing your clothing inside out. Make sure some tags are visible and that others can tell the clothing is on wrong. Bonus points for wearing your shirt backward too so that the tag is in front.

EASY BUTTON: Instead of inside out, wear clothing that stands out—neon and sparkles, here we come!

 **DOUBLE DARE:** For even more of a challenge, go to a store and try on clothing backward or inside out, then ask the store employee if they like the look.

 ## DARE 84 — PRACTICE THE PAUSE

Worry tells many of us that if we run out of things to say during a conversation, The Cringe will be so enormous that we'll just die of embarrassment.

Oh yeah, Worry? Let's test that prediction out.

Practice the dreaded PAUSE today and put an awkward pause in the middle of a group conversation. While hanging with others, start telling a story about class, your dog, or that family vacation you went on last week. Then, in the middle of the good part, just . . . drift off. You might even say . . .

Will it feel cringey? Absolutely. The real question is, how long does The Cringe last? And how quickly does the conversation resume?

 Observe a group conversation and watch for awkward pauses, like a joke that falls flat or a person who loses track of what they were saying. Then watch the group's response and see how long it takes for everyone to move on. Three minutes? Thirty seconds? Three seconds? Does the group give the Pause Culprit a hard time? Or does everyone shrug and move on?

 **PLAY HOT SEAT**

Put yourself on the spot with this Dare and get ready to blush. With a group of friends, cousins, or classmates, set a timer for three minutes and take turns sitting in the Hot Seat. When you're on the spot, others get the chance to ask you whatever questions they want. The Hot Seat is "hot" because it will feel a bit like being under a spotlight (and wow, stage lights are WARM!). It's like three minutes of Truth or Dare but with an all-truth lineup. Answer those questions as best you can, and when the timer goes off, it's the next person's turn to sit in the Hot Seat.

 Set a timer for 20 minutes and sit in a public place—a coffee shop, a sidewalk, the library—with a sign that says "Hello! Ask me anything." Parents, for safety and for fun, hang nearby for this one and prepare to be amazed by the burning questions of your local community and your child's brilliant answers.

178 • **The Be Brave Activity Book**

DANCE IN FRONT OF OTHERS

Put on some dancing shoes, embrace the music, and move those happy feet! Your challenge today is to dance in front of some about-to-be-adoring fans. Maybe you're a great dancer . . . maybe not so much. Well, for this Dare, it doesn't actually matter how good at dancing you are. In fact, less skill at dancing means more practice with getting a little embarrassed, which is your goal!

Who you dance in front of and how well you dance will change how tricky this Dare is. It's easier to get those feet moving with family on the packed dance floor of a wedding reception, and a bit harder in the quiet lobby of an office building! Pick two to three of the boxes below to boogie by. For extra credit, check all of the boxes!

	IN FRONT OF YOUR...				
	Besties	Classmates	Family	Teammates	Strangers
Dance with others also dancing around you					
Solo dance with your best moves					
Solo dance with your silliest moves					

 If you're not ready for your solo quite yet, track down a few friends and try flocking. In this game, four people stand in a diamond, all facing the same direction. The person at the top point of the diamond is the leader, just like the bird at the front of a flock of geese flying through the sky. When the song starts, everyone follows what the leader does, copying their dance moves. When the leader is ready to let someone else lead, they turn to the left or the right, toward another point of the diamond. Since the rest of the group will turn too, this puts someone else at the front of the flock, who is now the dance leader that the flock follows. If you play this game really well, it looks impressive. People will come up after the dance and ask how you all learned such a long and fancy dance routine.

 # SING IN PUBLIC

Birthdays are the best, aren't they? The happy people, the silliness, the fun, the cake! Channel a little of that good energy for this Dare and sing the song that everyone knows, where everyone least expects it. Head to a big, busy store or a quiet office lobby and sing "Happy Birthday." Will this draw attention? Yes. Will this confuse people? Probably. Will this also surprise and brighten someone's day? We'll see . . . Check out the sample Bravery Ladder below for ideas on how to make this Dare easier or more difficult:

BRAVERY LADDER

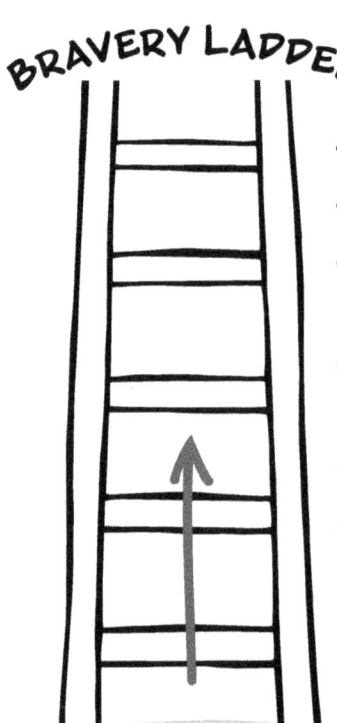

- Sing a full karaoke song solo—must include dancing and stage silliness!
- Sing a karaoke song on stage with friends, using a microphone.
- Sing "Twinkle Twinkle Little Star" solo in an office lobby or busy elevator.
- Sing "Happy Birthday" with someone else in an office lobby, where it is no one's birthday.
- Sing a song solo for friends while no music is playing.
- Sing "Happy Birthday" solo for a special Birthday Buddy.
- Sing a song out loud in the car with friends while a song is playing.
- Sing "Happy Birthday" as part of a group, preferably for someone's birthday.

 If "Happy Birthday" does not sufficiently show off your vocal range, go ahead and try karaoke. Go online and find some music without lyrics (YouTube or Spotify will have options), and be the rockstar you were born to be. Karaoke is usually performed in front of a crowd, but this Double Dare will be equally effective if you complete it in a public place where no one is expecting your beautiful rendition of "Hakuna Matata."

180 • The Be Brave Activity Book

MAIL A POTATO

For this Dare, send a friend a starchy surprise and mail a potato—without a box. Yes, really.

STEP 1: Get a potato. Uncooked, please.

STEP 2: Write a mailing address and return address in Sharpie on the potato. Add your message or artwork on the other side.

STEP 3: Go to the post office and hop in line.

STEP 4: Tell the post office worker, "I'd like to mail this potato please." Pay for postage.

STEP 5: Mail the potato.

Will it work? Maybe. Will the post office worker look at you funny? Probably. Will your friend be completely shocked? Very likely. Will it be hilarious? Almost definitely.

NOTE: If a spud does not give you enough space for your message or artwork, mailed vegetable upgrades include a butternut squash or a coconut. Just remember, heavier food = more postage.

Chapter 10 • Cringey Stuff (Embarrassment) • 181

 # REST IN PEACE IN PUBLIC

Need a break? Why wait? Get some rest and relax today—wherever you are. Lay down on the floor in a public place for a full minute without explaining to others why you're chilling on the ground. You may get some hellos, some funny looks, or even questions like "Are you okay?" You can smile and say "Yep, fine!" Then keep relaxing on that hallway, sidewalk, or elevator bay.

NOTE: If someone like a security guard specifically asks you to please move, you can end this Dare before the minute is up, but that's the only reason to get up before those 60 seconds have passed.

GO ON A BLUSHING BONANZA

When it comes to blushing and embarrassment, it's easy to end up getting stuck in a cycle. Feeling embarrassed makes you blush, but Worry says blushing guarantees others will notice that you are anxious or embarrassed . . . which makes you feel even more embarrassed . . . which makes you blush even more.

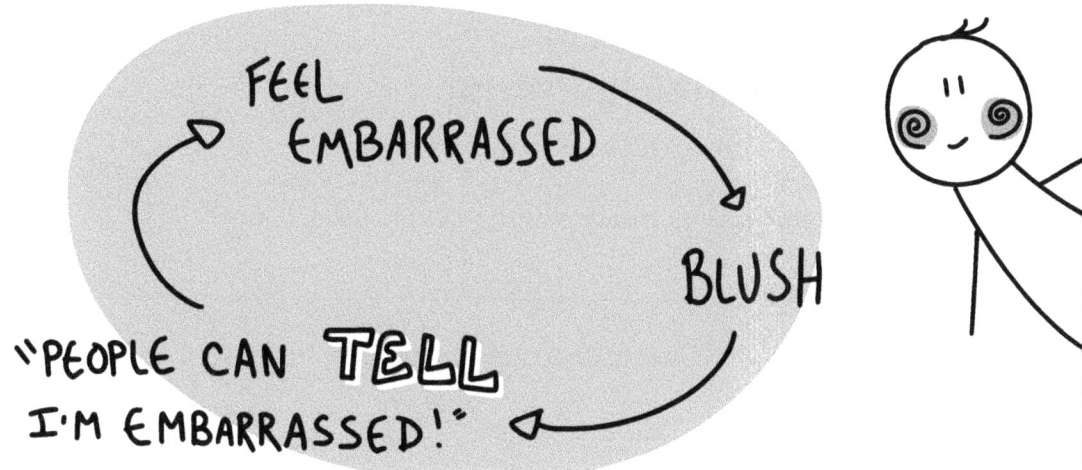

You can't control blushing—it's an automatic response, part of the body's alarm system turning on (see chapter 1). If you can't prevent embarrassment, and you can't stop the Blush, then you have to get confident that you can handle blushing in front of others. To test out whether it's the end of the world (or just a bump in the road) if others notice you blushing, this Dare asks you to get others to notice your blush *on purpose*.

STEP 1: CREATE A BLUSH.

Here are some options:

> **GOOD:** Rub your cheeks hard before talking to a group or presenting.
>
> **BETTER:** Use makeup to put a fake perma-blush on your cheeks.
>
> **BEST:** Purposely do something embarrassing that makes you blush IRL—share a cringey story, tell a bad joke, answer a question wrong, or mess up a name.

STEP 2: POINT IT OUT.

When you're talking, make sure others notice you're blushing by bringing attention to it. Try any of the following:

"Ugh, my cheeks are so red right now! I'm such a blusher."

"Check out this beautiful blush! So gorgeous, right?"

"Yikes, I'm going to turn so red right now."

Put your hands up to your cheeks and fan your face.

STEP 3: SEE WHAT HAPPENS.

Fill out the following with your observations:

Did others notice the blush when you pointed it out?

_____

What did they do? Smirk? Shrug? Ignore?

_____

How long did The Cringe last? Forever, or just for a moment?

_____

EMBARRASSMENT
BRAVERY BADGE

Check all those *DONE!* boxes?

CONGRATULATIONS! You have earned your Embarrassment Bravery Badge.

EXTRA CREDIT

Still want more? Try out a few Extra Credit Dares below:

- ➡ Make a mistake while presenting.
- ➡ Make fart sounds in a public restroom.
- ➡ Make a list of boring topics and text or talk about them.
- ➡ Order something that a restaurant clearly does not serve.
- ➡ Spray water under your arms to make it look like you're sweating.
- ➡ Cheer the loudest during a game.
- ➡ Yell across the hall to say hi to someone.
- ➡ Interrupt a group of people with a silly story.
- ➡ Stand facing the wrong way in an elevator.
- ➡ Challenge a stranger to a game of Rock, Paper, Scissors.
- ➡ Watch a cringey movie.
- ➡ Pay for a purchase entirely in coins.
- ➡ Drink something while making your hands shake on purpose.

CHAPTER 11
Not Knowing Stuff (Uncertainty)

I have a riddle for you.

I'm that annoying feeling you wish would go away before an important event where you care about the outcome. I'm the reason people say "You'll be fine" over and over. Crystal balls and fortune tellers are designed to eliminate me (but they never really do). My complete opposite is unattainable for all human beings on Earth. I am at the core of pretty much all Worry out there. If you actually got rid of me, you would be a god.

What am I?

ANSWER: Wouldn't you like to know?!

What Is Uncertainty?

Uncertainty is being not totally sure about something, whether that's the whereabouts of your dog or the color of your underwear today. If you've worked your way through any other chapters in this book, that feeling will sound very familiar because difficulty handling uncertainty is at the core of almost every anxiety out there. When a new situation shows up and you think:

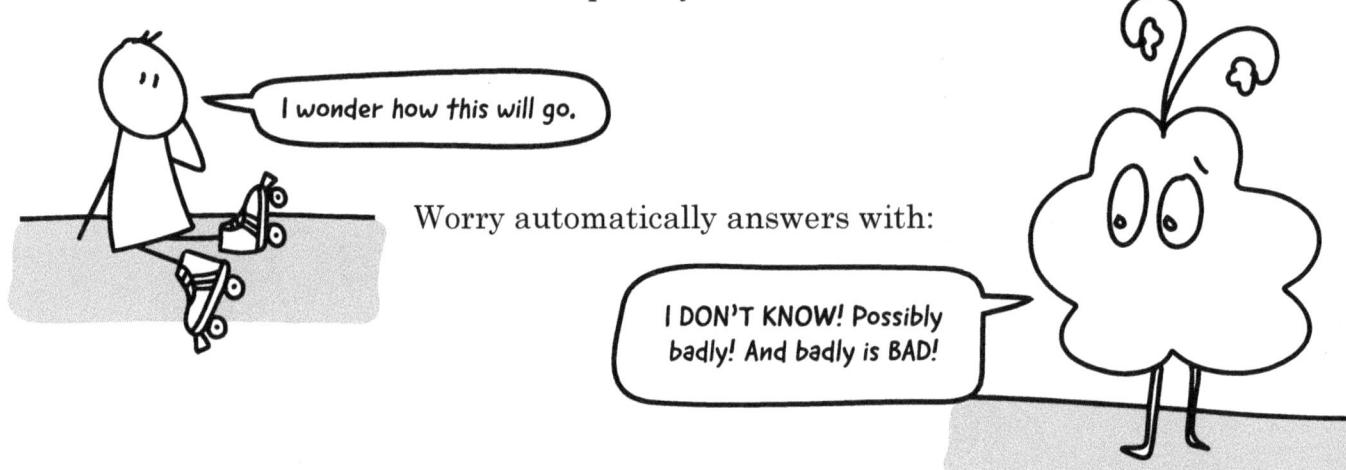

When it's too scary to think that things might go wrong, Worry will get you to work incredibly hard to try to make SURE things go right, or to make sure you don't risk things going badly at all.

Worry tells you that you must be 100 percent sure that you are safe, that things will be okay, and that everything will go the way you want. According to Worry, the possibility of an unpredictable situation or uncomfortable moment is just too much to bear. Even the tiniest doubt, a .0001 percent chance of catastrophe, is unacceptable. If you can't be SURE of something, then it's too risky—you better avoid it.

Most anxiety-provoking situations are scary precisely BECAUSE they are uncertain. You really DON'T know what will happen if you give that speech, or if you invite that new friend over, or if you pet that giant dog! It's that murky place called "the future," where you know nothing for sure.

Your brain is wired to anticipate all the bad stuff that *could* happen, no matter how unlikely, so you can be ready just in case. This means that when an unpredictable situation comes up, like a new activity or the chance to hang out with someone you've just met, your mind will generate all kinds of stories of the ways that it could go wrong. These stories are like the spooky stories told around a campfire—what makes those stories so scary is that you have no way to guarantee there is NOT a creepy masked dude with an ax lurking in the woods just beyond the shadows. You might be pretty darn sure that the story is pretend, but you can't see the whole woods, all at once, all the time. So even though you are fairly sure that nothing is out there . . . you just don't know.

Worry's Tricks for Uncertainty

Worry uses its usual arguments when talking about uncertainty, including trying to convince you that something unlikely but very bad will happen, or that you can't handle the feeling of not knowing. However, Worry's main move when it comes to uncertainty is to give you a case of the "what ifs."

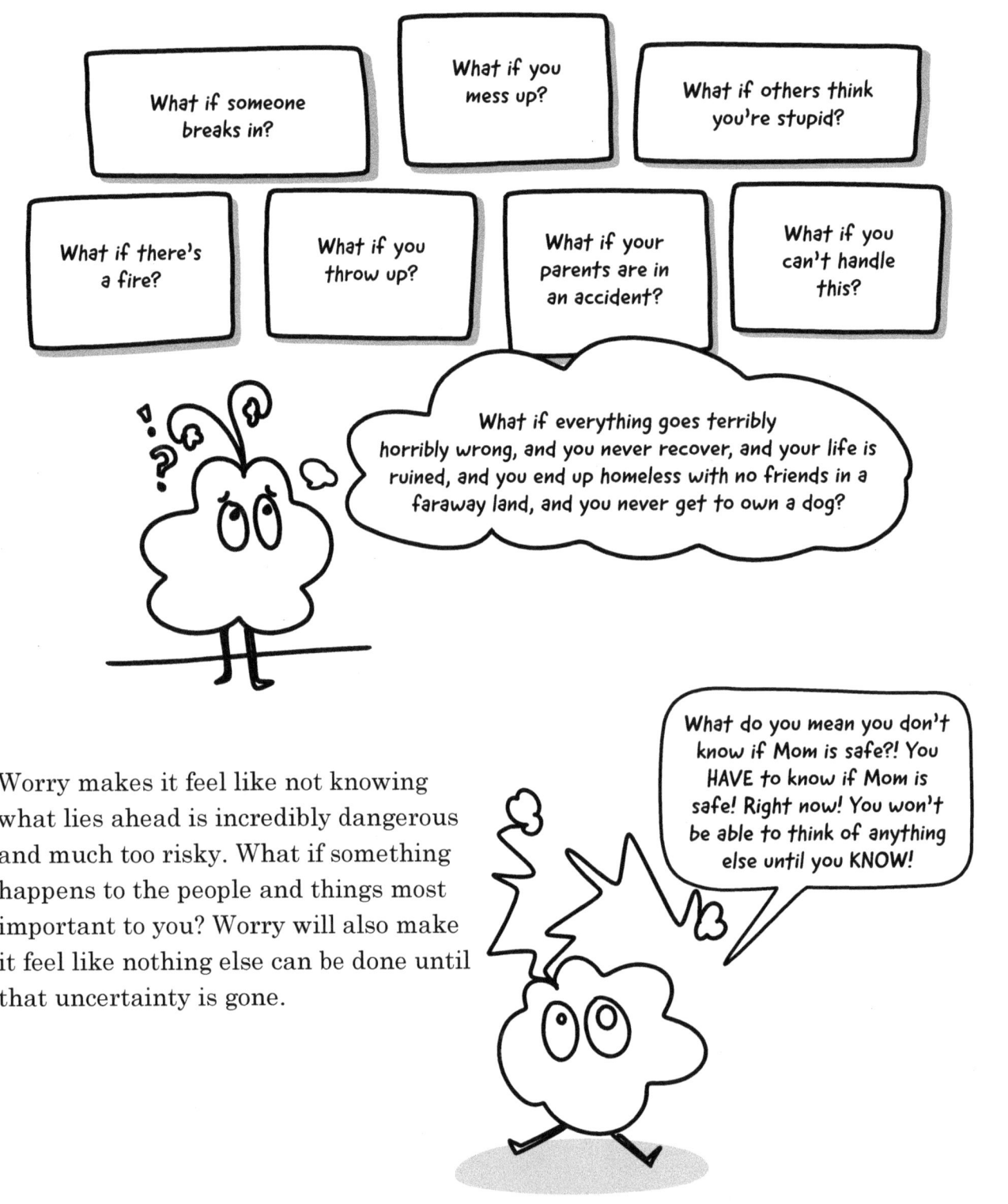

Worry makes it feel like not knowing what lies ahead is incredibly dangerous and much too risky. What if something happens to the people and things most important to you? Worry will also make it feel like nothing else can be done until that uncertainty is gone.

190 • The Be Brave Activity Book

WHAT ARE SOME OF THE "WHAT IFS" THAT WORRY FEEDS YOU?

IDK! IDK! IDK! IDK! IDK! IDK! IDK! IDK! IDK

IDK! IDK! IDK! IDK! IDK! IDK! IDK! IDK! IDK

Chapter 11 • Not Knowing Stuff (Uncertainty)

Worry's Demands for Uncertainty

Once Worry has tricked you into thinking about all the unpredictable things that *could* go wrong, it demands that you do everything necessary in order to be certain you have prevented these things from happening. In other words, Worry wants you to be 100 percent sure that everything will happen just as you expect it to.

CERTAINTY CHECKLIST

- ☑ Double-check to be SURE you made a good checklist!
- ☐ Don't eat that unfamiliar food to be SURE you won't throw up!
- ☐ Turn the key a third time to be SURE you locked the door!
- ☐ Text your parents once more to be SURE they are still safe!
- ☐ Ask Mom again to make SURE you know the exact schedule for the day!
- ☐ Stay away from spiders to be SURE they don't hurt you!
- ☐ Confirm with Dad where the birthday party is and who will be there to be SURE that you are prepared!
- ☐ Wipe down the table for the 21st time to be SURE you don't get sick!
- ☐ Think of 15 conversation topics ahead of time to be SURE you have something to say with your new friends!
- ☐ Don't talk in class to be SURE your classmates don't judge or criticize you!

There's just one problem with trying to be certain about everything in life . . .

The Secret Truth About Uncertainty

Although Worry wants you to be certain of everything all the time, here's a little not-so-secret secret:

⧽ BEING 100 PERCENT SURE IS IMPOSSIBLE. ⧼

The truth is, uncertainty is everywhere, every day. You cannot know what will happen in the future, whether it's five years from now or five seconds from now. Certainty does not exist.

You are not magic (right?), so you cannot possibly know *for sure* what will happen at that sleepover with your best friend. Yes, you might be pretty confident that you'll have a great time, since the 382 sleepovers you've had in the past have been fun. You might be 99.9 percent sure that you will eat pizza, watch a movie, stay up too late, and maybe sleep . . . eventually. But since the future hasn't happened yet, you can't say *for sure* that you won't end up eating tacos instead of pizza! Or sit on the roof watching the stars until 3 a.m. instead of watching that movie! You can't even guarantee that a giant unicorn won't walk through the front door and ask if you both want to go salsa dancing. (Note: If that happens, say yes.)

You also can't be sure that you won't tragically slip on a banana peel, hit your head, and get a concussion right before the best part of the movie. Or that a burglar won't break in while you are eating breakfast and steal your friend's epic sticker collection.

Fill in the bubbles with all the silly things you can think of that could possibly occur later today, even if they might not be very likely:

- A celebrity who might visit:
- A miracle that might occur:
- An animal that could be present:
- A dangerous thing that might happen:
- A place you might end up going:
- A thing that might explode:
- A thing your parent might do:
- A thing you might do:

What to Do Instead

Because uncertainty is *always* present, you need to practice doing stuff *in the face of uncertainty* on every day that ends in Y. If you can't be sure of anything, then you better get pretty darn good at handling being unsure.

Let's see. Days ending in Y. That would be . . . oh. I see. That's all the days.

The more you practice leaving a little uncertainty in your life, the easier it will be to participate in all the fun stuff and new situations where not knowing is part of the package. The Dares that follow will earn you a degree in IDK from WhoKnows University, although the school's reputation is pretty questionable.

Maybe you'll graduate . . . or maybe you won't. I guess you'll just have to wait and see . . .

Dad joke alert!

 **LIVE AN UNCERTAIN LIFE**

Intolerance of uncertainty is a lot like intolerance of an allergen—even the tiniest bit of uncertainty mixed into the day causes a big, puffy, red-eyed reaction. For kids who struggle with uncertainty, the slightest possibility of things not going well means that it feels necessary to prepare for and mitigate EVERY possible curveball that the family's schedule could throw at them. This need to control the day is a *safety behavior* (see the Pro Tip in chapter 6), and it tends to take the fun out of life, since even fun surprises become threatening when they are unexpected.

The Dares that follow are a great starting point for helping kids gain confidence in tolerating uncertainty. However, this is an area where daily practice will give you the best results. Just as small doses of an allergen can desensitize the immune system to that allergen over time, repeated doses of uncertainty each day will help kids react to those IDK moments with less and less intensity. With this in mind, your long-term goal should be to . . .

Sprinkle some IDK into your week: Try to add little moments of uncertainty to each day. Don't review every detail of every family member's schedule with your child. Flip the usual after-school routine without a heads-up. Leave a surprise block on the calendar (see Dare 93). Each time you leave a part of life as a question mark, your child will have a mini wave of uncertainty to ride and the opportunity to see that yes, they can handle not knowing. Make sure to celebrate and reward going with the flow for all those IDK moments too (Wing-It Points, anyone?). But keep in mind: Leaving a few life question marks for your kid will inevitably lead to kid questions.

Instead of answering . . .

Leave your child guessing: The truth is, no one knows exactly what the day will hold, and that's okay. With this in mind, leave some space for chance when talking about life and its calendar items by *not* answering every one of your child's questions with certainty. For example, try replacing "definitely" with "probably" when talking about the timeline for the day. This also means sharing mixed opinions for questions where there is no clear answer (You might say, "One part of me thinks X about that issue, but another part of me thinks Y"). As a parent, your goal is to be honest with your child and tell them the truth . . . and sometimes, the honest answer is "I'm not sure."
And perhaps most important . . .

Make like Elsa and *Let. It. Go*: While researchers are still uncertain (ha!) of how intolerance of uncertainty develops, many factors likely contribute to its development, including genetics, ingrained thinking patterns, environmental cues, and—*cough cough*—adult modeling. If you have a child with a white-knuckle grip on life's steering wheel, do a quick check to see if your little micromanager may be picking up on your own macromanager tendencies. For example, do you always have a plan A, plan B, and plan C/D/E for any outings? Order the same thing at restaurants every time you go? Decline to delegate things because others may not do it the way you think is best? Prepare for the worst, and expect . . . well, actually, the worst? If so, consider whether you might be unintentionally signaling to your child that uncertainty is unacceptable. If so, it's time to take steps to let go of the reins. Model acceptance of uncertainty: Go to the grocery store (*gasp!*) without a shopping list! Send that email without triple-checking the spelling! Take that beach vacation and leave some time unscheduled! Modeling acceptance of uncertainty is a "fake it 'til you make it" situation. By acting as if you are open to uncertainty, over time you actually will become more open to it.

Finally, remember . . .

If life throws you a curveball, go with the swerve: When you take risks and leave things to chance, sometimes things go wrong. This is okay. In fact, it's actually helpful because those curveballs are essential to your ultimate goal: building your child's confidence in their ability to handle whatever life throws at them (even the bad stuff). If you do head to that soccer practice without doing a gear check and end up forgetting the uniform, walk your child through the problem-solving necessary to keep moving and get back on track. Can you run home to get the jersey? Can your child start the practice without their uniform? Does it stop your kid from getting ice cream with the team afterward? When things go wrong and everyone still makes it through to the other side, your child has a chance to see that even when things don't go as planned, you can deal.

Uncertainty: Dares

DARE 91 — VISIT A NEW-TO-YOU ATTRACTION OR MUSEUM

Learn something new without knowing exactly what you'll be learning: Visit a new-to-you museum or other attraction. To increase the challenge, text Great-Uncle Eddie or another relative and have them pick the attraction you'll be visiting. You're allowed to look up the address, but no researching the visit ahead of time. It might be a terrible boring waste of a morning, or it might be your most favorite educational adventure ever. Or it might have moments of both stupidity AND awesomeness!

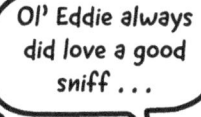

DARE 92 — WATCH AN UNFAMILIAR MOVIE

No preview? No problem. Take in a cinematic masterpiece or a so-bad-it's-good story and watch an unfamiliar movie. Parents are allowed to preview and confirm that the movie is age-appropriate, but they may not tell you any of the plot, the length of the film, or what happens at the end. Grab some popcorn and get ready to be transported to . . . somewhere! Where something happens! For some length of time!

DOUBLE DARE: Have your parents list three unfamiliar film options and choose the movie by title alone—no peeking at the cover art.

Chapter 11 • Not Knowing Stuff (Uncertainty)

DARE 93 — UNSCHEDULE YOURSELF

Does your calendar control you? Are you scheduled to within one inch of your life? Do you have to check your schedule 15 times a day? If so, this Dare is for you. Have an adult pick a day this week and put a "surprise" on the calendar by blocking off a chunk of time where you don't know exactly what will happen. It could be after school on a Tuesday, or it could be a Saturday afternoon. Your parents could plan something special, flip-flop everything on your schedule, or keep it totally ordinary. At home, at the park, at school . . . who knows? Your only job is to show up and go with the flow. If only the rest of life were that easy . . .

 **DOUBLE DARE:** Make it a whole day. Wacky Wednesday, Mixed-Up Monday, or Spontaneous Sunday, here we come!

DARE 94 — TRY IMPROV

Dust off your acting skills and get ready for a performance where no one knows what will happen ahead of time—not even the actors! Put on an improv show or play an improv game with your family or friends. Improv, short for improvisation, is a type of performance where there is no script. Usually, the audience helps direct what the show will be about. Try out one of the show or game options below.

 ### PUT ON A SHOW
Walk on stage (to great applause) and ask your audience to shout out topics they would like performed. Have them pick a person, then a place, then a situation. For example:

- Person: Aunt Edna
- Place: On the Moon
- Situation: Writing a Yelp review

Once you have all three, your job is to make up and act out a story based on the prompts! You can add some challenge by asking your audience to shout

out adjustments in the middle of your performance, then try to incorporate those changes into your show on the spot. Set a timer and see how long you can make your performance last!

PLAY SILLY SUPERHEROES
Have the audience describe a silly predicament the world is in. Maybe all the squirrels in your city suddenly decided to take over the post office, or scientists accidentally used up all the nacho cheese in their experiments and now the cheese-loving public is panicking. Then have your audience members select an unlikely superhero to try to save the day—you figure out how! Sticky-Fingers Fred to the rescue?

TELL A ONE-WORD STORY
Sit in a circle with at least two other people and tell a story, one word at a time. Everyone has to work together to tell a story that makes sense. Start with the classic: "Once" . . . "upon" . . . "a" . . . "time" . . . "there" . . . "was" . . . "a" . . . Spoiler: These are pretty much always ridiculous.

DRAW LINES FROM A HAT
Have everyone write down three random phrases and toss them all in a hat. Then start your scene. When someone calls out LINE, you have to pull a line out of the hat and incorporate it into your scene.

HAVE A QUESTIONS-ONLY CONVERSATION
Sit down with another person and try to have a full conversation using only questions. Set a timer and see how long you can keep your conversation going.

PLAY FORTUNATELY UNFORTUNATELY
Pair off with a partner or gather a group and tell a story one sentence at a time that toggles back and forth between fortunate and unfortunate events. Open your story with a situation, such as "One day, Anna the Rabbit was walking in the park and she tripped on a rock . . ." Then take turns telling the rest of the story: "Fortunately, she was able to stop herself from falling off the cliff . . ." "Unfortunately, the way she stopped herself was by bumping into a giant angry bear . . ." "Fortunately, the bear was blind and couldn't see where Anna was . . ." "Unfortunately, the bear was blind because it had lasers for eyes . . ."

> **EASY BUTTON:** Instead of performing, attend a show where there might be audience participation. Will the show be any good? Who knows! Will you get called on? Hard to say!

DARE 95 · MAKE IT A SINGLE-CHECK DAY

This Dare saves you time by getting rid of the extra checks that Worry demands you do. Make today a single-check day. For 24 hours, resist the urge to double-check (or triple-check) any of the following:

- Door locks
- Window shades
- Your backpack
- What's for lunch
- The schedule
- Your homework
- Your spelling
- Anything else you usually double-check
- This list

DARE 96 · HAVE A PARENT GO TO AN UNKNOWN LOCATION

Get unsure about your parent's location: Have a parent run an errand without telling you where they are going or when they will return. No location sharing on the phone, no text updates with an ETA, no communication whatsoever.

EASY BUTTON: Go with your parent on an errand but keep the destination(s) and timeline unknown.

 # SAVE UP YOUR QUESTION TOKENS

Ditch reassurance by limiting how often your family can answer questions today. Gather three hair ties, bracelets, or index cards: These are your question tokens. Anytime you want to ask your parents a question (1) that you've already asked, (2) that you *prooobably* know the answer to, or (3) with an answer that you can find yourself, you have to spend a Question Token to get an answer. Examples of questions that might cost a token include:

- Is it going to storm today?
- What time are we leaving again?
- Do I HAVE to go to school?
- When will Mom be home?
- How many fingers do I have?

Once your question tokens are gone, your parents are not allowed to answer any more reassurance-seeking questions for the day. They might reply with a canned response like "Already asked, already answered" or "Ooh, that's a good question! Save it for your next token."

Here's the best part: Resisting asking questions is hard work, and hard work deserves a reward, so if you save those question tokens and have a few left at the end of the day, you can trade those tokens in for a reward! Work with your parents to choose a reward ahead of time that feels exciting, and feel free to check out the ultimate reward list in appendix F for ideas.

Try this for a full week and earn a reward by saving up 10 tokens by the end of the week.

Chapter 11 • Not Knowing Stuff (Uncertainty) • 201

GO OFF THE GRID

Give your digital self a break and rest those hardworking typey-texty fingers: Spend a day with no phone or Wi-Fi. Yes, this will mean that you won't know if your friends texted you. Or if anyone called. Or if you got any new emails. It might feel spooky. But playing a game without interruptions or biking carefree through the world with no dings or distractions might also feel, dare I say, nice?

This challenge also means that for the day, you are without access to that search engine of certainty: Google. No looking up the answers to those random questions that pop in your mind. (No, your parents can't look it up for you either.)

Wondering what actor played the sheriff in your favorite show? Can't search that. Want to know how many teaspoons are in a gallon? Have to figure it out another way. Curious which animals eat their own poop? For today, you'll just have to wonder . . .

If no digital access all day feels daunting, try building up your confidence with the example Bravery Ladder below:

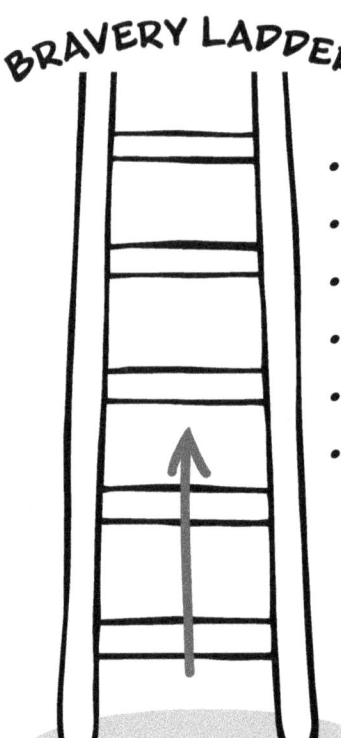

- Spend an entire day with no phone or Wi-Fi.
- Enjoy a five-hour break from all things digital on the weekend.
- Spend an afternoon at home with no Wi-Fi.
- Go on a fun family outing with no phone access.
- Take a morning off from texting (calls allowed).
- Spend an hour at home without access to a phone.

 **Don't tell any of your friends you're taking the day off—they might call! And you won't answer! Eek! Let's see what happens . . .**

 ## CHOOSE BY CHANCE

Make it so that even *you* don't know what you're going to do next! Spend the whole day making choices by flipping a coin. Red shirt or blue shirt? Flip. Pancakes or french toast? Flip. Read a little or draw a picture? Flip. Ride a wild horse or scuba dive with the dolphins? Flip.

See how many times in a day you can pick something by flipping that coin!

Goal: _____   Actual: _____

 ## DO AN UNCERTAIN DARE

No one on Earth knows what this Dare will be yet! Ask someone else to come up with a bravery-building Dare for you today, created just for you. Roll the dice, pick a number out of a hat, or use a random number generator on the internet to see who you will be asking to challenge you. Here are some people you can assign to each number:

1. Mom, Dad, or a grandparent
2. A sibling
3. Your best friend
4. A teammate or classmate
5. An aunt, uncle, or cousin
6. A teacher

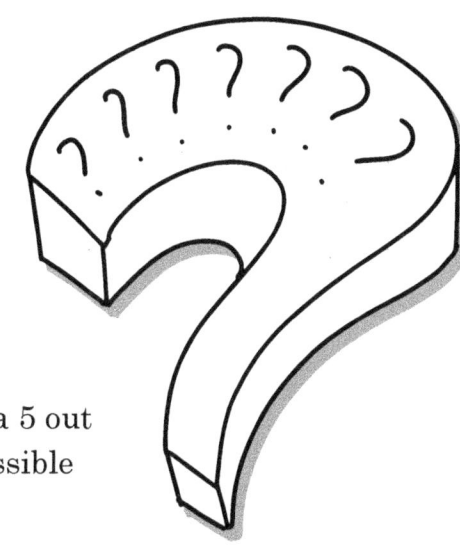

Let the person know that your challenge should be a 5 out of 10 on the difficulty scale—not easy, but not impossible either.

UNCERTAINTY BRAVERY BADGE

Check all those DONE! boxes?

CONGRATULATIONS! You have earned your Uncertainty Bravery Badge.

EXTRA CREDIT

Still want more? Try out a few Extra Credit Dares below:

➡ Roll a dice to decide what to eat for breakfast in the morning.

➡ Make a snap decision without confirming it's the "best" or "right" choice.

➡ Attend an event where you don't know what the timeline is.

➡ Leave the house without double-checking you have what you need.

➡ Take an alternate route to school or practice.

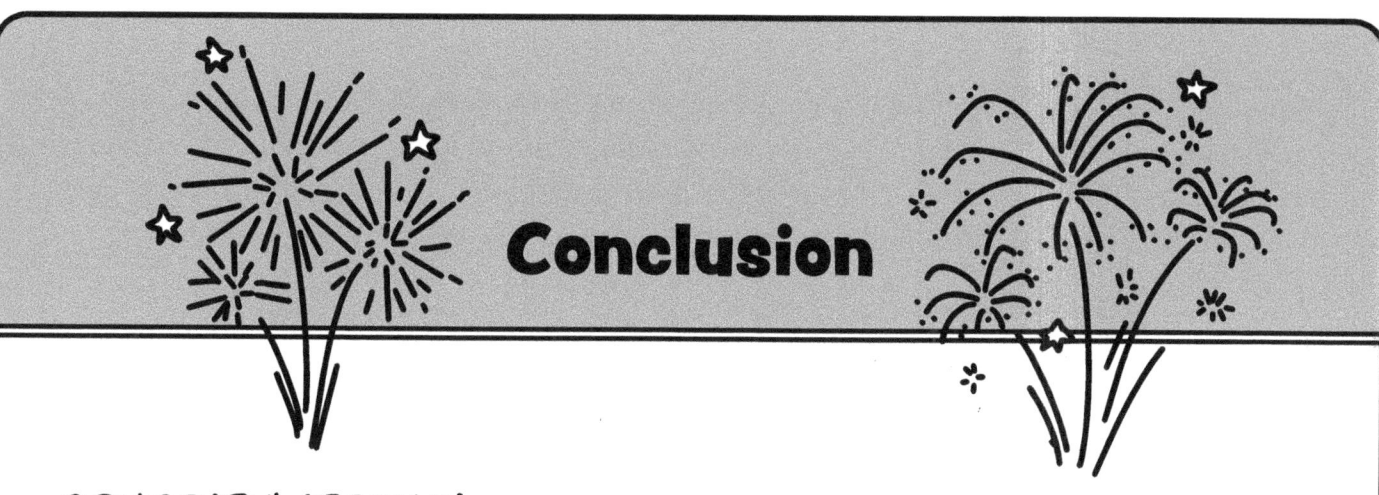

Conclusion

CONGRATULATIONS!

You made it to the end. By reading this book and learning more about how anxiety works, you've made yourself a wiser kid when it comes to Worry, and that's one of the most important things you can do to tackle anxiety.

If you went further and conquered even one of the Dares in this book, then kudos! You have taken steps toward facing your fears and exercised those Brave Muscles—that's absolutely worth celebrating.

If you've tried out the full set of Dares in a chapter, huzzah! You have trained for bravery, faced a common fear, and proved to yourself and everyone else that you can handle that spooky thing even if anxiety shows up. Flex those muscles and cheer!

If you completed all of the Dares in this book . . . WOW! Just wow. Congratulations on getting your black belt in bravery. You have challenged, confronted, and overcome Worry on all fronts, truly earning the title of Braver Kid. Well done.

So how do you guarantee that this newfound confidence and competence sticks around?

By continuing to practice, of course!

Like a runner who has trained for and won a race, you should feel great about the Brave Muscles you've built through all the Dares you've completed in this book. However, to keep the confidence you worked so hard for, you'll need to channel that inner athlete and continue to complete bravery workouts—this time by creating your own Dares in everyday life.

Whenever you're feeling anxious, challenge yourself to **Face It**—whatever "it" is—by taking the tools you've learned here and using them to keep those Brave Muscles strong. Even if Worry shows up, you know that it will stay in the backseat while you drive toward whatever fun and important thing comes next.

Best of all, when Dares become the norm and you take steps to face your fears every day, you go from *being* brave to *living* bravely. When you live bravely, your confidence explodes, infusing every part of your life. It becomes much easier to achieve your "next big thing" because no matter how hard that thing may be, you know beyond a shadow of a doubt that Worry can't get in your way.

> SO KEEP DARING MY FRIENDS, AND ENJOY THAT BIG BRAVE LIFE. I'LL BE CHEERING YOU ON!

—DR. KATHRYN

Chapter 11 • Conclusion • 207

APPENDIX

Appendix A: Dare Log

What you tried: _____

How spooky was it?: _____

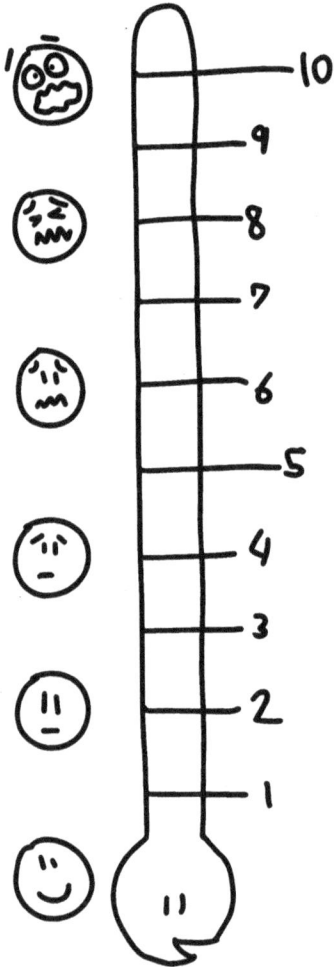

What you learned:

☐ The bad thing Worry said would happen didn't actually happen!

☐ The Dare was not as bad as Worry said it would be!

☐ It might have been hard, but I can totally handle it!

☐ Worry made it feel like this would be a big deal, but actually, it was a little deal!

☐ Even though it was scary, it was actually also sort of . . . fun?!

☐ Even if it was uncomfortable, this Dare was manageable!

☐ I am a beacon of awesomeness! 😊

☐ Other: _____

Appendix B: Blank Bravery Ladder

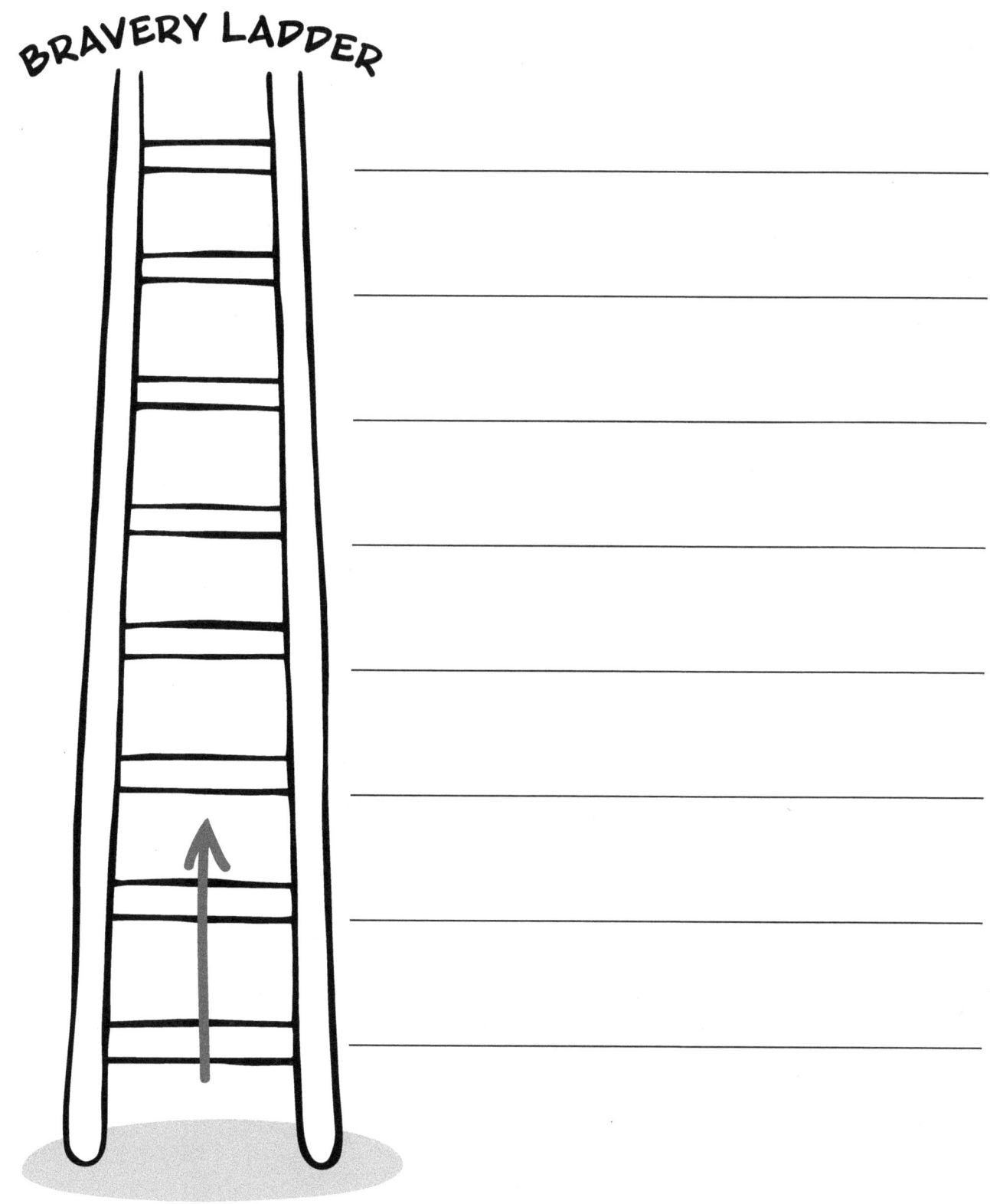

Appendix C: Reminder of How Awesome You Are

Not sure you can handle this Dare? Repeat after me:

"Just like the millions of other kids who have tried hard stuff and made it through, I CAN TOTALLY HANDLE THIS!"

Now let's make a plan to tackle this Dare. Here are some things you could put in your plan to help make the challenge feel manageable:

- A parent hanging out nearby
- A friend giving you a thumbs up from behind a tree
- A high five after you succeed
- Extra thick socks
- A coping phrase (like "I got this!")
- An encouraging text from Grandma
- A brave "power song" to listen to before you start
- A warm towel
- A *tiiiny* change to the challenge so it's easier at first
- A friend trying out the challenge with you
- A compass and flashlight
- A reminder to try slow breathing if your feelings get big
- Adventure goggles
- A reward at the end for trying your best
- Puppies . . . lots and lots of puppies

Copyright © 2025 Kathryn F. Hecht, *The Be Brave Activity Book*. All rights reserved.

WRITE YOUR PLAN HERE:

Appendix D: Tips for Parents on Rewarding Bravery

Reward systems involve the use of positive reinforcement to increase bravery-building behavior. Examples include setting up a token jar or sticker sheet so kids can log each Dare they complete. As I explain it to kiddos, "Being brave is hard work, and hard work deserves reward."

Common FAQs:

Q: Rewards for *this*? I don't know. I don't want to have to bribe my kid to do something that they should be doing already.

A: Understandable. No one wants to have to resort to bribery to get a child to behave. However, I've got great news: Reward systems are, in fact, not bribery at all. Bribery is trying to persuade or coerce someone into doing something that you want by giving a gift beforehand. For example:

- Giving the judge those Knicks tickets before the sentencing to encourage him to award a lenient sentence
- Slipping the official a $20 bill in the hopes that she approves your visa paperwork
- Wiring the fighter a bunch of cash before the match and asking him to throw the fight
- Giving your kid a candy bar in the car and saying "Now you have your treat, so PLEASE BE GOOD when we get to the nursing home with Great-Aunt Mildred! Just like you said you would, okay?!"

Positive reinforcement is not a bribe but a *paycheck*, something given *after* an action is completed to honor and reward that hard work. For example:

- Taking your child to a Knicks game after a year of perfect attendance
- Slipping your employee a $20 coffee gift card as thanks for her extra hours of effort sorting through visa paperwork
- Wiring the fighter a bunch of cash as agreed after his training pays off and he wins the fight
- Giving your kid that candy bar *after* a successful and well-behaved visit to the nursing home to visit Great-Aunt Mildred

When you think about what it takes for a child to be brave—tolerating some very uncomfortable physical sensations, risking the feeling of judgment or embarrassment, exercising the herculean self-control necessary to not bolt in the face of fear—it becomes obvious that this is definitely hard work and is thus worthy of reward.

Q: Okay, what should I reward?

A: Like the paycheck for a long and hard day of work, most people offer rewards for actions that are important, but also difficult and/or uncomfortable. This *perfectly* describes what you are asking anxious kids to do. Consider a child with separation anxiety: You are asking that child to walk into the party alone despite the wave of nausea, pounding heartbeat, and an almost uncontrollable, neurologically hardwired urge to run back to their parents and cling for dear life. Yikes. Difficult? Check. Uncomfortable? Check. Still super important? Check!!!

Positive reinforcement is not only much more effective than a bribe, but it also models how our wider world works. The "Hard Work = Reward" equation plays out in a million other ways throughout a child's life:

- The hard work of homework earns the reward of good grades.
- The hard work of keeping good grades earns the reward of acceptance to choice colleges.
- The hard work of practicing piano over and over and over earns the reward of a great recital.
- The hard work of introducing yourself to new people earns the reward of new friendships.
- The hard work of facing adversity earns the reward of confidence and resilience.

Q: Okay fine, but then won't I have to reward my kid for *every little thing* from now on? Not into that.

A: Again, understandable. No parent wants their kids to be spoiled or entitled. We certainly don't want little Billy believing that he should earn rewards for every little thing. The goal is not to turn your child into someone who says "I'll put my sock on if it gets me a cookie!" or "I'll be nice to the neighbor kid today if you buy me that LEGO set!" No.

Hard work does deserve a reward, but the keyword here is *hard*. If the action is easy, there is no need to reward it. When you reward brave behavior, it is because the behavior is difficult, causes uncomfortable feelings, and requires significant effort on the part of the child. When you ask an anxious child to go to school, you are asking that they use *all* of their self-control to walk through those school doors. They also have to exercise that iron will while tolerating a tidal wave of really uncomfortable physical symptoms (thanks, False Alarm Feelings). Same goes for climbing the high dive ladder, going to that party with unfamiliar people, and staying in bed alone in the dark. That is all absolutely hard work.

The good news? Hard work eventually turns into easy work if your child practices it enough. The high dive turns into no big deal and school drop-off goes from monstrosity to meh. And when a brave action is no longer hard work, you no longer need to reward it. You can instead reevaluate what earns that paycheck. Perhaps, now, rewards are only given for bravely jumping off the even-higher dive, riding the dreaded bus to school instead of getting dropped off, or independently going to bed. The best part? When you reward the hard work of bravery, you end up with even more confident kids in the process.

If you're not sure what might be motivating, ask your kid to read through appendix F: The Ultimate Rewards List.

Appendix E: School Refusal Playbook

If your child is refusing school, try this four-step process to move them toward attendance and participation.

1. **Confirm the reason(s!) for school refusal.**

   While Worry is one culprit for the word *no* at 7:26 a.m., it may not be the only culprit. School refusal happens for four reasons. It can be an attempt to:

   - Avoid situations or events that trigger uncomfortable feelings like anxiety or sadness—things like separation from a parent, fire drills, friend drama, and other not-fun stuff
   - Avoid social or evaluative situations like tests, group work, or the lunchroom
   - Get parent attention (five hours with Mom running errands, anyone?)
   - Get external rewards like video game time, also referred to as "Bonus Saturday"

   Questions to ask in order to get to the bottom of this include:

   - How did this behavior develop over time?
   - Did any notable events occur right before the school refusal started?
   - Is your child willing to attend school if a parent is there?
   - What does your child do when at home on a school day?
   - What are school environment triggers?

   Once you know why the refusal is happening, it's time to . . .

2. **Take steps to address those reasons.**

   To start, remind your child that it's okay to feel anxious at school. Make a plan with your child for what will happen if they become nervous during the school day, including ways to reset with some slow breathing, a drink of water, or a brief check-in with school staff. Keep in mind that this should not be a check-in with a favorite person or a free pass to go to a "fun" place in the building, but just a few minutes to practice that all-important skill of self-regulation.

   Next, take action on the specific reason for school refusal:

   - **For avoidance of uncomfortable feelings:** Practice handling the feelings and the situations that are hard. This might mean practicing separation at home first, practicing listening to a fire alarm sound and going through the motions of a drill, or even practicing with smoke alarms at home! Figure out what's hard or spooky, and practice in order to help your child feel more confident in their ability to handle the situation when it arises.
   - **For avoidance of social and evaluative stuff:** Encourage your child to take small, manageable steps to practice these very situations. If the fear is rooted

in social interaction, try a few of the Dares from chapter 2. Have an anxious tester on your hands? Try practicing a handful of timed tests online. The thing to remember is that even though social worries feel like an emergency, they are not. The more you signal your confidence in your child's ability to handle these situations, the faster they will gain that confidence themselves.

- **For attention-seeking behaviors:** Minimize the attention you give to refusal behavior. Now is not the time for hours-long heartfelt conversations about why skipping school is a bad idea. When a kid says no to going to school, keep your reply warm, short, and sweet: "I know it's hard, but I know you can handle this, just like the other kids at your school." Keep an eye out for any kids or school staff that might be giving refusal behavior a lot of attention too. Then make sure that the hard work of attending school gets rewarded. You can reward your child with tangible reinforcers, like a favorite snack on the way home or an attendance points system. (For those of you hesitant about reward systems, note that almost every school has some form of reward for consistent attendance and other good school behaviors! See appendix D for more.) You can also reward this hard work with the most effective reinforcer of all: your attention. Don't be shy about expressing how proud you are when your child takes the plunge and hops in the car!

- **For external rewards outside of school:** Reduce access to fun stuff outside of school. Tighten the net on what your child is able to do at home on a school day. This may mean turning off the Wi-Fi and changing the password or taking the controllers for a video game console. It may mean increased supervision by a parent. Whatever the benefits of being at home on a school day, your goal is to limit those as much as possible. You want to make consequences for non-attendance outweigh the benefits. Make sure there are clear consequences for missing school, which leads to step 3 . . .

3. **Make attending school more rewarding than staying home.**

How? Make sure a refused school day is *much* less fun than an attended school day by making staying home as boring as possible. For most kids, this includes:

- Still having to wake at their weekday time, do their morning routine, and pack their backpack
- Sitting at the kitchen table and doing make-up schoolwork all day—not even a recess!
- No access to privileges—no TV, video games, or phone
- No naps; no going in their room
- No after-school activities; no friends coming over later
- No attention from parents

4. **Make sure to give your child multiple chances to say "Yes" to school (or at least another chance to say "Ugh, fine").**

   Remember, your primary goal with school refusal is always physical presence at the school, as much as possible. This is particularly important with anxiety-driven school refusal. The longer that a student is able to avoid an anxious situation or location like school, the stronger the anxiety about that situation becomes. This means that the longer your child is out of school, the more fearful they will become and the more difficult facing that fear will be.

   The good news is that it's hard to be bored and anxious at the same time. Often, after the wave of anxiety has faded from the initial refusal and boredom has set in, kids reconsider their willingness to attend. After all, school has some good things too, like friends, recess, and even the occasional fun activity. If your child is at home, maximize your chances of at least some attendance by asking, "Are you ready to go to school?" once per hour.

For more support around school refusal, check out these excellent resources by school refusal expert Dr. Christopher Kearney:

- Kearney, C. A. (2021). *Getting your child back to school: A parent's guide to solving school attendance problems* (Rev. ed.). Oxford University Press.
- Kearney, C. A., & Albano, A. M. (2018). *When children refuse school: A cognitive-behavioral therapy approach—parent workbook* (3rd ed.). Oxford University Press.

Appendix F: The Ultimate Rewards List

- Sleep in for ___ minutes
- Have 20 extra minutes of computer time
- Have 20 extra minutes of video games
- Get a backrub
- Choose game for game night
- Enjoy some craft time
- Have parents email a relative about your success
- Get an extra song at bedtime
- Get an extra story at bedtime
- Get a foot rub
- Go for a walk
- Have lunch with parent(s)
- Paint parent's nails
- Paint own nails
- Pick a silly thing for an adult to do
- Pick dessert
- Play a board game
- Play on parent's phone
- Put on a shadow puppet show
- Stay up late
- Enjoy a sweet treat
- Watch a special movie
- Watch a special TV show
- Wear a piece of adult jewelry, tie, or watch
- Download a song
- Decorate cookies
- Download a game
- Download an app
- Pick a trinket from a mystery grab bag
- Buy a book on kindle
- Buy a new toy
- Buy new LEGO pieces or building set
- Enjoy a "Get out of trouble free" card
- Get curfew extended by 30 minutes
- Take the car to school instead of the bus
- Drive the "good" car
- Enjoy a night off setting the table
- Use the phone at the dinner table
- Enjoy priority computer access
- Enjoy priority TV access
- Go to a skate park
- Go roller skating
- Act as the DJ at dinner
- Have a backyard picnic
- Take a break from siblings
- Eat breakfast in bed
- Go camping in the backyard
- Go camping in the living room
- Choose the next family day adventure
- Get a chore pass
- Cook a secret dish for the family
- Decorate paper placemats
- Dictate what route is driven home
- Put on a family talent show
- Fly a kite
- Get to be "only child" for a day
- Go biking
- Go to the beach
- Go into the city
- Go to a pet store
- Go to the bookstore
- Go to the library
- Go to the park
- Help cook
- Have a living room picnic
- Make a fort
- Make sailboats from backyard items
- Enjoy a night off dish duty
- Get permission to play in mud

Copyright © 2025 Kathryn F. Hecht, *The Be Brave Activity Book*. All rights reserved.

- Get permission to jump on the couch or bed
- Pick your seat at the table
- Pick your seat in the car
- Pick the next dinner
- Pick the next family movie
- Pick where you sleep
- Have a picnic in the park
- Play ball with parent(s)
- Play dress-up
- Write a sidewalk chalk greeting on the porch
- Have a special placemat at dinner
- Bake a cake
- Go on a scavenger hunt
- Take photos and print them
- Go fishing
- Go out for ice cream
- Go swimming
- Buy a book at the bookstore
- Go ice skating
- Go out to lunch
- Go bowling
- Go out to a movie
- Go out to eat
- Go to a museum
- Go to the zoo
- Go camping
- Go to an amusement park
- Play all-house lights-out hide-and-seek
- Play all-family ghost in the graveyard
- Have an all-family water balloon fight
- Have an all-family snowball fight
- Have an all-family Silly String fight
- Have an all-family Nerf gun fight
- Create your own fancy shaving cream beard (or one for a parent)
- Put a whipped cream pie into an adult's face
- Host a pizza party
- Host a potluck
- Have a sleepover party
- Make s'mores
- Take your shoes off for the day
- Have no chores for a day
- Pick out your favorite cereal at the grocery store
- Have a photo shoot in a photo booth
- Book a one-hour headshot photo shoot
- Drink a fancy drink out of a pineapple or coconut
- Have a tropical night (umbrella drinks, luau music, tropical movie on beach towels)
- Visit a farmers' market
- Make ice cream floats
- Go watch the sunrise over a lake
- Go kayaking or paddleboarding
- Go snow tubing
- Visit a trampoline park
- Visit an arcade
- Play mini golf
- Tie-dye a T-shirt
- Go to a drive-in movie
- Go to a baseball game
- Go late night stargazing
- Have a family LEGO building competition
- Go to the airport and watch the planes land
- Make a cardboard robot costume (and battle!)
- Eat pancakes for dinner
- Play "messy" Twister (dyed shaving cream on each dot)
- Play spitball target practice/spitball Olympics
- Have a shaving cream party: Fill a sink with a can of Barbasol and get wild
- Do a secret agent hallway obstacle course with streamers or string as "lasers" you can't touch

Copyright © 2025 Kathryn F. Hecht, *The Be Brave Activity Book*. All rights reserved.

About the Author

KATHRYN F. HECHT, PHD, is a mom, licensed child psychologist, speaker, parent coach, rock climber, pizza lover, and bravery cheerleader. A partner at Anxiety Treatment Resources in MN, Dr. Kathryn started out by doing research on how scary and stressful stuff impacts how kids develop. She published a few papers, but what she actually learned from all that work was that kids can handle really hard things, and that all kids can be brave if they get the chance. She decided to spend her career helping kids be brave, and helping other grown-ups help kids too. Dr. Kathryn presents both locally and nationally on pediatric anxiety/OCD and exposure-based CBT. She can pretend to be a grown-up for about 20 minutes before she reverts to a goofy 9-year-old. She might be eating pizza right now.

More Great Books for Kids from  PESI Publishing

Fiona McPhee, Please Listen to Me!

Dr. Katie Hurley, LCSW.

A confident, creative girl learns how to harness her assertive nature into strong leadership, celebrating the strengths and contributions of her classmates.

Let's Grow on an Adventure

Lauren Mosback

An anxious young boy gains confidence by exploring the many wonders of nature, his worrisome thoughts growing smaller and smaller with each new discovery.

The Not-So-Friendly Friend

Christina Furnival, MS, LPCC

Children learn an easy and practical lesson about how to firmly and assertively–yet kindly–stand up for themselves in the face of a bully.

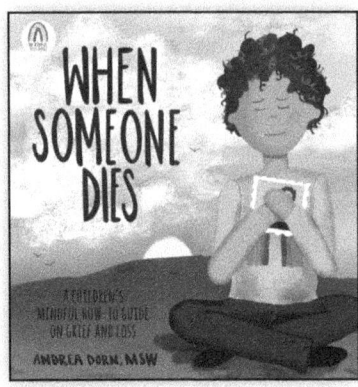

When Someone Dies

Andrea Dorn, MSW

Through the lens of mindfulness, children learn how to say goodbye after a loss, make space for any emotions that arise, and work through their grief.

Welcome to Therapy

Andrea Dorn, MSW, LISW-CP

This book walks children through the process of starting therapy in simple, concrete, and developmentally appropriate terms so they can better understand what to expect.

The Small and Tall Ball

Frank J. Sileo, PhD

Oliver feels excluded from his school's "Mother-Son & Father-Daughter Dance" because he has two dads. But then he and his classmates find a way to celebrate diverse families of all kinds.

pesipublishing.com | Follow us on Instagram: @pesipublishing